BeeUe NiiEe

THE CURTAIN THAT DIVIDES US
A METAPHOR FOR SOCIETY'S PERPETUAL INEQUALITIES.
MESSAGE FOR THE YOUTHS

The Curtain That Divides US: A metaphor for society's Perpetual Inequalities.
Message for the youths

The Curtain That Divides US: A metaphor for society's Perpetual Inequalities. Message for the youths

Copyright © 2024 by BeeUe NiiEe
All rights reserved.
No part of this book may be reproduced or used in any manner without the prior written permission of the copyright owner, except for the use of brief quotations in a book review.

Disclaimer
This is a work of fiction. Names, characters, businesses, places, events, and incidents are either the products of the author's imagination or used in a fictitious manner. Any resemblance to actual persons, living or dead, or actual events is purely coincidental.

License Notes
This book is licensed for your personal reading only. This book may not be re-sold or given away to other people. If you would like to share this book with another person, please purchase an additional copy for each person you share it with. Thank you for respecting the hard work of this author. No part of this publication may be reproduced, distributed, or transmitted in any form or by any means, including photocopying, recording, or other electronic or mechanical methods, without the prior written permission of the publisher, except in the case of brief quotations embodied in critical reviews and certain other non-commercial uses permitted by copyright law.

ISBN 979-8-9897518-4-6 (Paperback)
ISBN 979-8-9897518-5-3 (Hardcover)
Also available in eBook and Audio formats

ResearchOnce, USA

*The Curtain That Divides US: A metaphor for society's Perpetual Inequalities.
Message for the youths*

Read the following book by the author:

The Curtain That Divides US: A metaphor for society's Perpetual Inequalities.
Message for the youths

To the youths, minorities, and advocates for change.

*The Curtain That Divides US: A metaphor for society's Perpetual Inequalities.
Message for the youths*

The Curtain That Divides US: A metaphor for society's Perpetual Inequalities.
Message for the youths

PREFACE

Imagine a curtain, unassuming and delicate, yet laden with profound implications. This curtain, which separates the economy and first-class sections aboard a commercial airline flight, is a powerful metaphor for the divisions within our society. It reveals the enduring inequalities that persist and underscores the systemic burden that the Black people in America continue to bear, casting light on the shortcomings we must confront.

On one side of this flimsy barrier lies comfort and privilege. Legroom abounds, and service is at your beck and call. Here, society bestows automatic respect upon occupants. The flight attendants, meticulously chosen and impeccably uniformed, cater to their needs. Physically, these passengers are no different from those on the other side—the economy or coach class. They possess the same human features. The distinction? Affordability. How they acquired their position matters little. The curtain does not care

The Curtain That Divides US: A metaphor for society's Perpetual Inequalities.
Message for the youths

about their earnings or the means by which they arrived. It only marks their place at that moment. Beyond this spot, these individuals blend seamlessly with the rest of humanity—until another occasion propels them into a privileged class.

Our society thrives on stratification, a phenomenon as ancient as humanity itself. We grapple, strive, and yearn to ascend the ladder, seeking our place within these divisions. Though seemingly insignificant, the curtain echoes the broader societal structure—a structure that inspires hard work yet perpetuates stratification. But there's hope. As the curtain flutters, it beckons to the younger generations. It calls upon them to recognize their role in narrowing the gap. For within its folds lies not just separation, but also the potential for change.

The boarding process commences with the announcer's voice echoing through the airport terminal: "Group one—the elite class, active military personnel. Are invited to board at this time." These privileged few strides forward, the first to ascend the rungs of societal stratification—at least according to most airlines. The announcements continue, calling each group, until we reach the group-less, the "classless," if you will. For this latter category, often

The Curtain That Divides US: A metaphor for society's Perpetual Inequalities. Message for the youths

labeled as group 7 or simply "group-less," boarding occurs after the initial groups. Often lacking overhead space for their hand luggage, these individuals face a different reality. They are required to check their bags—for free.

In the space, front of that flimsy curtain—where the privileged reside—lies abundance: plentiful meals, respect, cozy blankets, and attentive care. The overhead compartments offer more room, accommodating larger and multiple pieces of carry-on luggage. But this is not merely about luggage logistics; it is about the broader implications of social class. Here, where the elites board, flight attendants exhibit greater tolerance. It is a coveted realm, especially for those who cannot afford it.

Yet, amidst this divide, there is a glimmer of hope—the youth. Those capable of enlisting in the military find themselves in a unique position. They can join the active military group, announced alongside the elites and first-class passengers. Unlike wealth, this group is not just earned; it is fueled by desire and devotion—the promise to protect our nation with their lives. These are the true heroes, deserving of honor beyond the curtain.

Listen closely, young ones, for this message transcends

The Curtain That Divides US: A metaphor for society's Perpetual Inequalities. Message for the youths

color and circumstance. Your destiny lies within your grasp—choose your class wisely. Picture it: the airplane boarding process. In front of that flimsy curtain, a world of privilege awaits. Will you sit there, where abundance reigns? Or will you remain on the other side, where scarcity looms? Imagine being among the first to board—the elite class, the privileged few. Here, there's room aplenty for hand luggage, meals are abundant, and seats are one and a half sizes larger. Society bestows upon its occupants a status and dignity that mere words cannot convey. But how does one gain entry?

The path is varied; some ascend through corporate achievement, while others bear the badge of active military service. Inheritance, too, catapults individuals into this coveted group. And then there is the hard-won route—the sweat, tears, and relentless pursuit of excellence. Whichever path you choose, belonging to this elite class is worth every effort, especially in your youth.

Yet, I confess, my thoughts sometimes veer toward categorization—race, education, privilege. But education and privilege cannot be discerned by outward appearance alone. So, I resort to the myopic labels: white or black. A simplification it seems

The Curtain That Divides US: A metaphor for society's Perpetual Inequalities.
Message for the youths

until we tally the benefits bestowed upon those on the other side of the curtain. Across society, group 1 enjoys opportunities—whether deserved or not—alongside justices meted out with a delicate hand of "mercy", the better interest rate on loans, the higher valuation of property, better support and promotion at work, better pay per unit work, easier access and discounted rates for services, lesser traffic violation, lesser penalties, and fees, better medical care despite paying less. For wealth accumulation, insurance adjusters extend their favor. Yes, too many benefits to mention— oh! The comfort of belonging! But let us not oversimplify. Each class is a mosaic— a blend of races, a tapestry of lives. The ratio defies easy categorization. So, young ones, choose your seat wisely. The curtain may be flimsy, but its implications are profound.

    The path to the coveted boarding group remains elusive for many—a labyrinth of challenges, an unequal playing field. These challenges form the essence of this book, "The Curtain That Divides US: A Metaphor for Society's Perpetual Inequalities. Message for the Youths." How difficult is it to transition to the elite class? How effortless to occupy the other side of that flimsy curtain? Perhaps you belong to a particular race, and as you contemplate,

The Curtain That Divides US: A metaphor for society's Perpetual Inequalities.
Message for the youths

memories replay like a movie—scenes visible only through your mind's eyes. You measure yourself against a coworker you once trained, who now strides ahead, promoted with corporate protection. Their egregious act overlooked. The inequity gnaws at you—the hurdles faced by you and your peers as you strive for the next rung. It is a daunting, arduous climb.

Yet, history whispers strength. You have studied your ancestors' triumphs and read of their struggles for freedom. The fight to be acknowledged as more than a "boy," more than a "thing," more than a mere "reproductive machine." Perhaps you've heard tales that leave you wondering how. "The Curtain That Divides Us: A metaphor for society's Perpetual Inequalities. Message for the youths" beckons you—a call to your own journey.

To the youths, we convey a message of empowerment and hope. You possess the energy, enthusiasm, and determination needed to challenge the status quo and spearhead change. By raising your voice, advocating for equal educational opportunities, and supporting initiatives that strive for educational equity, you can contribute to breaking down the curtain and creating a fairer world for all.

The Curtain That Divides US: A metaphor for society's Perpetual Inequalities.
Message for the youths

Find your path to that seat in front of the curtain. Blunt the otherwise sharp edges of enduring disparities and combat the inequalities. And as you ascend, extend a hand to those just starting their climb. Bring the ladder closer and steady their grip on the rails. For in unity lies our collective ascent.

BeeUe NiiEe

The Curtain That Divides US: A metaphor for society's Perpetual Inequalities.
Message for the youths

TABLE OF CONTENTS

Preface v

Introduction 1

Chapter 1: The Curtain of inequality 5

    Understanding inequality: A historical perspective 5

    The origins of inequality in society 7

    The impact of inequality on different generations 9

    The multi-dimensional nature of inequality 12

    Economic Inequality: The wealth gap 14

    Social Inequality: Discrimination and Prejudice 21

    Social inequality: Plea deals for minorities 27

    History of racially motivated credit discrimination 34

    Racial discrimination in Credit and Taxes 39

    Educational inequality: Access and Quality 49

    The invisible Barriers of class 52

    The effects of segregation and gentrification 54

The Curtain That Divides US: A metaphor for society's Perpetual Inequalities. Message for the youths

The role of gender and intersectionality 57

The curtain of inequality: How it divides us 59

Chapter 2: Empowering the youth to break the curtain. 62

How youths can combat societies inequalities 62

The power of education: A Tool for Equality............... 64

Improving Access to quality education........................... 67

Addressing Educational Disparities 69

Encouraging lifelong learning... 72

Youth activism: Amplifying voices for change.............. 74

The importance of Youth Activism in history 77

Tools and platforms for youth advocaCy....................... 80

Building solidarity and collaborative movements 82

Building resilience and confidence in the face of inequality .. 85

Developing self-awareness and empathy........................ 87

Overcoming stereotypes and self-limiting beliefs 90

Nurturing leadership and civic engagements skills 92

Chapter 3: Breaking down the Curtain: Strategies for all ages 95

Promoting economic equality and financial literacy 95

Reducing the wealth gap and income inequality 97

Strengthening social safety nets 99

Empowering individuals through financial education 101

Addressing social inequality: Challenging Discrimination 104

Promoting inclusive policies and legislation 106

Fostering diversity and inclusion in communities 108

Encouraging empathy and understanding 110

Creating an equitable society: Policy and systemic changes 113

Advocating for fairness in education systems 115

Rethinking criminal justice and prison reform 117

Promoting equal opportunities in employment 120

Chapter 4: Rising above the curtain: Inspiring stories of Change 123

Youth-led initiatives: making a difference 123

Success stories of youth-led movements 126

Lessons learned and strategies for success 128

Sustaining and scaling up youth initiatives 130

Intergenerational collaboration: Bridging the Gap 133

The Power of intergenerational mentorship 135

Collaborative solutions for inequality 137

Empowering all ages through mutual support 139

Celebrating progress and inspiring hope 142

Recognizing positive change and achievements 144

Inspiring individuals and communities to take action 146

Conclusion: Breaking the chains of inequality: Our collective responsibility 149

SECTION II – 152

The Cost of Inequality: Examining Racial Wage Gaps in Healthcare, Finance, and Technology 152

Introduction: Significance of wage disparities 153

Chapter I: Understanding wage Disparities 158

Definition and Measurement of Wage Gaps 158

Factors contributing to wage disparities 160

Historical context of racial wage gaps 162

Impacts of wage disparities on minorities 165

Chapter II: Wage disparities in healthcare 168

Overview of the healthcare industry 168

Racial wage gaps in healthcare: statistics and trends... 170

Factors Affecting Wage Disparities in Healthcare 172

Case Study: Examining Racial Wage Gaps in Medicine 175

Ethical Considerations in Addressing Healthcare Wage Disparities 177

Chapter III: Wage Disparities in Finance 180

Overview of the Finance Industry 180

Racial wage gaps in finance: statistics and trends 182

Factors Affecting Wage Disparities in Finance 184

Case Study: Examining Racial Wage Gaps in the California Health Care Sector 186

Strategies for Reducing Wage Disparities in Finance . 189

Chapter IV: Wage Disparities in Technology 193

Overview of the Technology Industry 193

Factors Affecting Wage Disparities in Technology 195

Case Study: Examining Racial Wage Gaps in Technology 197

The Curtain That Divides US: A metaphor for society's Perpetual Inequalities. Message for the youths

Promoting Diversity and Inclusion in the Tech Sector200

Chapter V: Policy and Interventions 203

Existing Policies and Interventions Addressing Wage Disparities 203

Evaluating the Effectiveness of Current Initiatives 205

Recommendations for Policy Changes 208

Promoting Equity and Equality in the Workplace 211

Chapter VI: Conclusion 214

Summary of Findings 214

Implications for Future Research 216

Final Thoughts and Call to Action 218

References 222

*The Curtain That Divides US: A metaphor for society's Perpetual Inequalities.
Message for the youths*

The Curtain That Divides US: A metaphor for society's Perpetual Inequalities.
Message for the youths

INTRODUCTION

Perpetual inequality weaves a palpable division throughout American society. Imagine the metaphorical airline curtain, separating first-class from economy. This curtain mirrors the societal divide. It symbolizes privilege and scarcity, echoing a broader structure. Though seemingly insignificant, the curtain echoes the broader societal structure—a structure that inspires hard work yet perpetuates stratification. Those that have all the privileges and those that simply do not because they cannot afford it. Our society thrives on stratification, a phenomenon as ancient as humanity itself. We grapple, strive, and yearn to ascend the ladder, seeking our place within these divisions until a certain population realize the difficulty in transitioning to the front of the curtain.

The boarding process commences with the announcer's voice echoing through the airport terminal: "Group one—the elite class, active military personnel. Are invited to board at this time." These privileged few strides forward, the first to ascend the rungs of societal stratification. The announcements continue, calling each group, until the last category, often labeled as group 7 or "group-less,'". Often lacking overhead space for their hand luggage, these individuals face a different reality.

On the other side of that flimsy curtain—where the privileged reside—lies abundance: plentiful meals, respect, cozy blankets, and attentive care. The overhead compartments offer more room, accommodating larger and multiple pieces of carry-on luggage. But this is not merely about luggage logistics; it is about the broader implications of social class. Here, where the elites board, flight attendants exhibit greater tolerance. It is a coveted realm, especially for those who cannot afford it.

Minorities across the globe encounter discrimination and marginalization that separates them from the majority. Contrary to popular belief, wielding power to subjugate others isn't solely the domain of majorities. In reality, minority elites, who amass wealth, often hold sway over societies. This book does not focus on the wealthy versus the poor or elites versus ordinary citizens. Rather, it delves into the systemic design that perpetuates inequalities—a deliberate scheme that subjects certain individuals to perpetual disadvantage. These people, who significantly contribute to the nation's functioning through indirect taxation and labor, often lack recognition. Instead of dismantling these barriers, society erects

The Curtain That Divides US: A metaphor for society's Perpetual Inequalities.
Message for the youths

curtains that divide us.

Throughout American history, Black individuals have carried the weight of developing the very foundations that underpin the nation's wealth. From the earliest days of slavery in the 17th century—where they toiled in tobacco and rice fields—to their contributions in constructing railways, historic landmarks, and other critical infrastructure, African Americans have been instrumental in sustaining America's prosperity. These enslaved individuals literally built America with their sweat and blood.

During the era of slavery, their labor was overtly exploited. They endured physical beatings, sexual assault, and forced procreation to bolster the workforce for their owners. They were bought and sold; their lives commodified for profit. Female slaves existed solely to serve the desires of their masters.

Fast forward to today, and the exploitation continues, albeit in more subtle ways. African Americans still bear the brunt of labor and economic burden. The mechanisms are covert: higher fees, elevated taxes, increased premiums, and steeper penalties. They receive meager services despite making higher payments. Property valuations fluctuate—lower when convenient for the "masters" and higher when it comes to tax assessments. This modern-day slavery perpetuates a cycle of poverty, ensnaring African Americans in its grip.

But there's hope. As the curtain flutters, it beckons to the younger generations. It calls upon them to recognize their role in narrowing the gap. For within its folds lies not just separation, but also the potential for change. *To the youths, your task is enormous and arduous, but you carry the hopes of your fore bearers—that there comes a day when you will live in a country where your efforts would be equally rewarded irrespective of race or color of skin or background.* Understanding your task should first start with recognizing what needs corrected. And then to what you must do to gain the necessary authority to close the gap of inequalities. "The Curtain That Divides US: A metaphor for society's Perpetual Inequalities. Message for the youths" chronicles the inequalities and highlights a proven path to transitioning to the front of the curtain on the commercial airline where lies plenty, more room, care, and respect. Choose your seat —in front of the curtain or behind the curtain? Choose to board first and sit in front of the curtain; strive to bridge the gap of inequality.

CHAPTER 1: THE CURTAIN OF INEQUALITY

UNDERSTANDING INEQUALITY: A HISTORICAL PERSPECTIVE

To address and combat the enduring inequalities that exist in our society, it is crucial to first understand the historical roots of these disparities. This subchapter aims to provide an insightful look into the origins and evolution of inequality, shedding light on the factors that have contributed to its persistence. By delving into history, we can gain a deeper understanding of the complex web of social, economic, and political forces that continue to shape our world today.

Throughout history, societies have been marked by various forms of inequality, such as wealth disparities, gender discrimination, racial segregation, and social class divisions. These inequalities have often been perpetuated through unjust systems and structures that favor certain groups while marginalizing others. Understanding the mechanisms that have enabled inequality to persist is essential for devising effective strategies to dismantle these oppressive systems.

The Curtain That Divides US: A metaphor for society's Perpetual Inequalities.
Message for the youths

One key aspect to consider is the role of power dynamics in shaping social hierarchies. Throughout history, those in positions of power have often sought to maintain and reinforce their privileged status, leading to the creation of systems that perpetuate inequality. By examining historical examples, such as feudalism, slavery, and colonialism, we can see how power imbalances have been used to exploit and oppress certain groups, while consolidating wealth and influence in the hands of a few.

Moreover, understanding the historical context in which inequality has evolved allows us to recognize the progress that has been made over time, as well as the persistent challenges that remain. From the suffrage movement to the civil rights movement, individuals and communities have fought tirelessly for equal rights and opportunities. While significant strides have been made, more work is needed to achieve true equality for all.

For the youth, understanding the historical perspective of inequality is especially crucial. By learning from the past, young people can gain insight into the struggles and victories of those who came before them, empowering them to continue the fight for a more just and equitable society. It is through education and awareness that the next generation can challenge the systems that perpetuate inequality and work towards a future where everyone has an equal chance to succeed.

Understanding inequality from a historical perspective is essential for addressing the enduring disparities that exist in our society. By examining the roots and evolution of inequality, we can gain insight into the mechanisms that have allowed it to persist. This knowledge empowers individuals of all ages to act, fight for justice, and work towards a more inclusive and equal tomorrow.

THE ORIGINS OF INEQUALITY IN SOCIETY

In the fabric of our societies, inequality is deeply woven, perpetuating a division that divides individuals based on their social status, wealth, and opportunities. To truly understand this enduring issue, we must delve into the origins of inequality and examine how it has shaped our societies throughout history.

From the dawn of civilization, inequality has been present in various forms. In ancient times, it was often linked to the unequal distribution of resources, where a select few held power and controlled the wealth while the majority struggled to survive. Feudal systems and caste hierarchies further entrenched inequality, as birth determined one's position in society, limiting mobility and perpetuating a cycle of disadvantage.

The Industrial Revolution brought about significant changes, as societies shifted from agrarian to industrial economies. While this led to advancements and improved living conditions for some, it also created a new class divide. The emergence of the bourgeoisie and the proletariat highlighted the growing wealth gap and the exploitation of workers. As capitalism thrived, so did inequality, with those at the top amassing unimaginable wealth while the working class continued to struggle.

Colonization is another key factor in the origins of inequality. European powers colonized vast regions, pillaging resources and exploiting indigenous populations. The ramifications of this imperialistic pursuit, such as the slave trade and forced labor, continue to shape inequalities today. The scars of colonization remain, with marginalized communities enduring historical injustices.

In recent times, technological advancements have ushered in a new wave of inequality. The digital divide separates those who have access to information and technology from those who do not, perpetuating educational and economic disparities. Additionally, gender and racial inequalities persist, with women and minority groups facing systemic barriers and discrimination.

Understanding the origins of inequality is crucial for empowering all ages to fight against it. By examining the historical context and acknowledging the systems that perpetuate inequality, we can challenge the status quo and work towards a more equitable society. *The youth, in particular, hold immense potential to drive change and dismantle the barriers that divide us.*

Through education, awareness, and collective action, we can rise above the curtain of inequality. By addressing systemic issues, advocating for social justice, and promoting inclusivity, we can create a society where opportunities are not limited by one's background or circumstances. It is up to all of us, regardless of age, to come together and fight for a future where everyone has an equal chance to thrive.

THE IMPACT OF INEQUALITY ON DIFFERENT GENERATIONS

Today, inequality continues to be a pressing issue that affects individuals of all ages. From the youngest members of our community to the elderly, the consequences of inequality are far-reaching and have a profound impact on every aspect of our lives.

In this subchapter, we will explore how inequality affects different generations and the urgent need for all ages to come together and fight against it.

For the younger generations, growing up in an unequal society can have lasting effects on their future opportunities and well-being. Children from disadvantaged backgrounds often face limited access to quality education, healthcare, and basic resources, placing them at a significant disadvantage from an early age. This inequality in early development can perpetuate a cycle of poverty and hinder their chances of upward mobility in the future.

Moreover, inequality can also impact the mental and emotional well-being of young people. Constant exposure to societal disparities can lead to feelings of hopelessness, low self-esteem, and increased levels of stress and anxiety. These negative emotions can have detrimental effects on their overall development and hinder their ability to reach their full potential.

In contrast, the impact of inequality on older generations is equally significant. Many seniors face economic hardships, lack of access to proper healthcare, and social isolation, particularly those who belong to marginalized communities. The gap between the rich and the poor widens as individuals age, leading to a greater risk of poverty and limited resources during their retirement years.

Furthermore, the intergenerational impact of inequality cannot be overlooked. The cycle of inequality often passes from one generation to the next, perpetuating a never- ending cycle of disadvantage. This not only affects individuals but also weakens the fabric of our society. It is crucial for all generations to recognize the importance of breaking this cycle and working together to create a more equitable society.

To address these challenges, it is essential for people of all ages to come together and fight against inequality. The younger generation must be empowered through education and mentorship programs, providing them with the tools they need to overcome the barriers imposed by inequality. Simultaneously, older generations can contribute their wisdom and experience to advocate for policies that promote equality and social justice.

Inequality has a profound impact on individuals of all ages, perpetuating disadvantages and hindering social progress. By recognizing the intergenerational consequences of inequality, we can work towards building a more equitable society for all. It is only through collaboration, understanding, and empowerment that we can rise above the curtain of inequality and create a brighter future for generations to come.

THE MULTI-DIMENSIONAL NATURE OF INEQUALITY

Inequality is a complex and multi-faceted issue that permeates every aspect of our lives. It goes beyond just the division of wealth and resources; it encompasses social, economic, and political disparities. Understanding the various dimensions of inequality is crucial for individuals of all ages, as we must work together to combat its pervasive effects.

One of the key aspects of inequality is social inequality, which refers to the unequal distribution of opportunities, resources, and privileges based on factors such as race, gender, and socio-economic status. It is disheartening to see how certain groups face systemic discrimination and are denied equal access to education, healthcare, and employment opportunities. By recognizing the existence of social inequality, we can strive to break down the barriers that perpetuate these injustices.

Economic inequality is another facet of the issue that cannot be ignored. The gap between the rich and the poor continues to widen, leading to a host of problems such as poverty, inadequate healthcare, and limited upward mobility. It is essential that we address the root causes of economic inequality, such as unfair tax policies and unequal distribution of resources, to create a more just and equitable society.

Political inequality is yet another dimension that impacts individuals of all ages. The concentration of power in the hands of a few can lead to the marginalization of certain groups and the suppression of their voices. By empowering ourselves and advocating for inclusive and representative governance, we can challenge the status quo and ensure that everyone's rights and interests are protected.

For the youth, in particular, understanding the multi-faceted nature of inequality is vital. "The Curtain That Divides US: A metaphor for society's Perpetual Inequalities. Message for the youths" serves as a reminder of the work that needs to be done. *Young people have the power to challenge the existing structures, to demand change, and to create a more inclusive future. By educating themselves about the various dimensions of inequality, they can become effective advocates and agents of change.*

Inequality is a multi-faceted issue that affects individuals of all ages. By acknowledging the existence of social, economic, and political disparities, we can work towards dismantling the barriers that perpetuate inequality. Empowering all ages to fight inequality is not just a moral imperative; it is essential for the progress and well-being of our society as a whole. Let us rise above the curtain of inequality and create a world where everyone has an equal opportunity to thrive.

ECONOMIC INEQUALITY: THE WEALTH GAP

In today's world, economic inequality has become an increasingly pressing issue that affects people of all ages and backgrounds. However, the wealth gap, specifically, refers to the unequal distribution of wealth within a society. However, evidence buttress, as a matter of fact, that blacks in the American society bear a disproportionate wealth gap due to deliberate systemic institutional deprivations and treatment. This section aims to shed light on this pervasive problem and provide insights into its causes and consequences, with a particular focus on the enduring inequalities in society and the messages it holds for the youth.

As we look around, we see a stark contrast between the haves and the have-nots. The rich seem to get richer while the poor struggle to make ends meet. This growing wealth gap not only undermines the principles of fairness and justice, but it also hinders social progress and stability. It is essential for all ages to understand the implications of this issue and work towards bridging the gap.

The causes of economic inequality are the uneven distribution of resources and opportunities and the all-around pervasive systemic discriminatory practices that the Black people endure. Factors such as education, access to healthcare, job opportunities, unfair taxes, and fines contribute significantly to one's ability to accumulate wealth. Unfortunately, these resources are not equally accessible to everyone. Let us explore the systemic barriers that perpetuate economic inequality, such as discrimination, lack of social mobility, and limited economic policies.

Workplace discrimination

The issue of racial inequality in the workplace is a complex and sensitive topic. According to a study conducted by U.S. News & World Report, the workplace environment in the United States is marked by significant racial disparities. The study surveyed workers from different racial and ethnic backgrounds and asked them whether they had experienced any form of unfair treatment at work in the past five years. The results showed that Black workers faced the highest level of discrimination, with 42% of them reporting such incidents. Asian workers also reported a high rate of unfair treatment, at 26%. Hispanic or Latino workers were slightly below the average, at 21%. White workers, on the other hand, reported the lowest rate of unfair treatment, at 12%. The study highlights the need for more effective policies and practices to promote diversity, equity and inclusion in the workplace and to combat racial bias and discrimination (Smart, 2021).

McKinsey & Company reports that Black workers are underrepresented in senior leadership and executive roles in the private sector, with only 4% of SVP level positions held by Black workers (Connley, 2021). The same report also concludes that Black workers are 23% less likely to say they receive "a lot" or "quite a bit" of support to advance at work, 41% less likely to view promotions in their workplace as fair, and 39% less likely to believe their company's diversity and inclusion efforts are effective, compared to their white counterparts working at the same company.

According to a Citi report, the US economy could have gained $16 trillion in the last two decades if the racial gaps in income, education, housing, and investment were eliminated. The report reveals that the Black pay gap alone contributed to a loss of $2.7 trillion in economic activity. It also shows that Black men earn only 71 cents for every dollar earned by white men, while Black women earn only 63 cents for every dollar earned by white men (Losey, 2016).

These reports suggest that there is a significant disparity between Black and white workers in terms of promotion and pay. However, it is important to note that the issue of racial inequality is multifaceted and cannot be fully addressed by a single study or report. It requires a concerted effort from all stakeholders to create a more equitable and inclusive workplace for everyone.

Discriminatory property tax assessment

A recent study by Brookings Institution revealed a significant racial disparity in the local property tax system. The study found that Black-owned homes are over-assessed at a higher rate than white-owned homes, resulting in a 10% to 13% higher tax burden for the average Black homeowner. This inequity contributes to the racial wealth gap and undermines the economic security of Black families. The study calls for reforms to ensure fair and accurate property assessments and tax policies (Fields, et. al,

2023).

Discriminatory property valuation

A Redfin study revealed that over the past 10 years, homes in predominantly Black areas have been consistently undervalued by tens of thousands of dollars compared to similar homes in white areas, even after controlling for fundamental factors that affect home values, such as square footage and walkability. The average home in a predominantly Black area across the country is worth $46,000 less than a comparable home in a predominantly white area. This gap reflects the economic cost to Black families of historical and ongoing racist housing practices, such as redlining, racial discrimination in mortgage lending and appraisals, and inherent racism (Anderson, 2021).

According to a study by Freddie Mac, the appraisals of homes in Latino and Black neighborhoods are more likely to be lower than the agreed-upon price of the property than in predominantly white areas. The study found that 15.4% of appraisals in Latino neighborhoods and 12.5% in Black neighborhoods were below the contract price, compared to 7.4% in majority-white neighborhoods. This discrepancy could have significant implications for homeownership and wealth accumulation among minority groups, as well as for the fairness and accuracy of the appraisal industry (Alfonseca, 2021).

The analysis shows that homes in Black neighborhoods are consistently undervalued compared to homes in white neighborhoods, even when they have the same size. This is a serious issue that needs to be addressed, as it affects the economic opportunities and stability of Black Americans. The undervaluation of homes in Black neighborhoods is not only unfair, but also detrimental to the overall health and wealth of the nation (Delgado & Ortegren, 2023).

Discriminatory traffic ticketing

The Crime & Justice Research Alliance conducted a study that revealed racial disparities in traffic ticketing. The study showed that Black drivers, who make up about 31% of the driving population, got 58% of the traffic tickets issued, while white drivers, who represent nearly 50% of the driving population, got only 36% of the traffic tickets issued. The study also indicated that Blacks are more than 2.5 times more likely to get a ticket than Whites. It implied that Black drivers face more ticketing than white drivers.

The study also raised concerns about the possible use of racial profiling by police officers to target minorities (Dunn, n.d).

The consequences of the wealth gap are far-reaching and affect individuals, communities, and the society as a whole. It leads to increased poverty rates, limited social mobility, and diminished economic growth. Moreover, it breeds social unrest and perpetuates a cycle of disadvantage for future generations. By understanding the consequences, we can collectively strive for change and work towards a more equitable society.

For the youth, this subchapter serves as a call to action. It highlights the importance of recognizing the enduring inequalities in society and empowers them to become agents of change. By educating themselves, engaging in social activism, and advocating for policy reforms, the youth can play a vital role in narrowing the wealth gap. This subchapter provides specific messages and actionable steps that young people can take to contribute to a fairer and more inclusive society.

Economic inequality and the wealth gap are critical issues that demand our attention and action. By understanding the causes and consequences of this problem, we can strive towards a more equitable future. This subchapter aims to inspire all ages, particularly the youth, to rise above the curtain of inequality and work towards a society where everyone has equal opportunities to thrive and succeed.

SOCIAL INEQUALITY: DISCRIMINATION AND PREJUDICE

In today's society, social inequality remains a pervasive issue that affects people of all ages, genders, races, and backgrounds. Discrimination and prejudice continue to create barriers and perpetuate divisions, preventing individuals, particularly the minority Black people, from reaching their full potential. In this subchapter, we delve deeper into the roots of social inequality, shedding light on the ways in which discrimination and prejudice manifest in our daily lives.

Discrimination takes various forms, from overt acts of racism or sexism to more subtle biases that shape our perceptions and interactions. It is crucial for individuals of all ages to understand the different manifestations of discrimination and recognize that it can impact anyone, regardless of their background or social status. By fostering awareness and empathy, we can begin to challenge and dismantle these unjust systems.

Prejudice, on the other hand, refers to preconceived notions and stereotypes that people hold about others based on their race, ethnicity, gender, or any other characteristic. These biases often stem from ignorance and fear and can lead to exclusion, marginalization, and unequal treatment. By addressing and challenging our own prejudices, we can create a more inclusive and equal society.

Through personal stories, case studies, and historical examples, this subchapter aims to inspire readers of all ages to confront social inequality head-on. By understanding the ways in which discrimination and prejudice shape our society, we can develop the tools necessary to fight against these injustices. It is essential for youths, in particular, to be aware of the enduring inequalities that exist and to become advocates for change.

From policing and justice system discrimination to poor healthcare service for black women during childbirth, social injustice pervades the aura of blacks. The following are some documented examples of the various forms of discrimination and prejudices confronting the blacks in our society.

Criminal Justice System

The National Conference of State Legislatures published a report on racial and ethnic disparities in the criminal justice system (NCSL, 2022). The report highlights data, reports, state laws, innovations, commissions, approaches, and other resources addressing racial and ethnic disparities within the United States' justice systems. It shows that Black people are disproportionately incarcerated.

A Pew Research Center survey revealed a large gap in the perceptions of racial bias in policing and criminal justice between Black and white adults. The majority of Black adults (84%) reported that Black people are generally treated less fairly than white people by the police, while only 63% of white adults agreed with this statement. Similarly, a high proportion of Black adults (87%) expressed the view that the U.S. criminal justice system is unfair to Black people, compared to 61% of white adults who shared this opinion (DeSilver, et al., 2020).

According to a study conducted by The Sentencing Project, a non-profit organization that advocates for criminal justice reform, there is a significant racial disparity in the incarceration rates of Americans. The study revealed that Black Americans are almost five times more likely to be incarcerated than white Americans, while Latino Americans are 1.3 times more likely to be incarcerated than white Americans. The study attributed this disparity to various factors, such as racial bias in law enforcement, prosecution, sentencing, and post-conviction policies, as well as socioeconomic inequalities and systemic racism that affect the opportunities and outcomes of people of color in the United States (Rezal, 2021).

Racial discrimination is a pervasive problem in many sectors of society, including the restaurant industry and law enforcement. A research report by the Crime & Justice Research Alliance revealed that Black drivers are more likely to receive traffic tickets than White drivers, even though they make up a smaller proportion of motorists. The report showed that Black drivers comprised 31% of the driving population, but received 58% of the traffic citations, while White drivers accounted for 49% of the driving population but received only 36% of the traffic citations. This indicates that Black drivers are overrepresented in traffic enforcement and face a higher risk of being fined or arrested than White drivers.

The report also suggested that this disparity may reflect implicit or explicit bias among police officers, as well as structural factors such as the location and frequency of stops. Additionally, there is evidence to suggest that Black people are more likely to be treated unfairly in restaurants, such as receiving poorer service, lower quality food, or being asked to pay in advance. These forms of discrimination can have negative impacts on the well-being, dignity, and economic opportunities of Black people (Horowitz, Hurst & Braga, 2023).

Poor Service in Stores and Restaurants

The Pew Research Center conducted a study on the experiences of Black and White Americans in stores and restaurants. The study revealed that Black Americans are more likely to report being treated unfairly in these settings than White Americans. According to the study, 35% of Black Americans said they have faced unfair treatment in stores, while 24% of White Americans said the same. Likewise, 21% of Black Americans said they have faced unfair treatment in restaurants, while 18% of White Americans said the same (Brewer, 2020, Jones & Lloyd, 2021). These studies suggest that Black Americans are more likely to be treated unfairly in restaurants and other public places (The Associated Press, 2018).

Healthcare during Childbirth

Discrimination suffered by Black women during childbirth is a serious public health issue that has persisted for decades in the United States. Black women are three to four times more likely to die from pregnancy-related causes than white women, and they also have higher rates of preterm births, low birthweight births, and severe maternal morbidity. These disparities are not explained by biological differences, but by the effects of systemic racism, inequality, and discrimination that affect every aspect of Black women's lives and health (Minooee, 2023).

Black women face multiple barriers to accessing quality maternity care, such as lack of insurance coverage, poverty, transportation challenges, and provider shortages. They also experience racial bias, stereotyping, and disrespect from health care providers and staff, which can lead to delayed or denied care, inadequate pain management, and lower satisfaction with their care. For example, report found that Black women were repeatedly ignored, dismissed, or coerced when they expressed their needs or preferences during childbirth. These negative experiences can have lasting physical and psychological consequences for Black women and their babies, Minooee concludes.

This subchapter emphasizes the importance of unity and solidarity in the face of social inequality. By recognizing that the curtain that divides us is merely a construct, we can work together to dismantle it and build a society that values diversity and equality. This message is especially crucial for the youth, who will shape the future and have the power to break down the barriers that perpetuate social inequality.

This is a call to action for individuals of all ages to confront and challenge the discrimination and prejudice that perpetuate social inequality. By understanding the root causes and manifestations of these issues, we can work collectively to create a more just and equitable society. It is our hope that this subchapter will empower readers to rise above the curtain of inequality and become agents of change.

SOCIAL INEQUALITY: PLEA DEALS FOR MINORITIES

In the American justice system, the guilty and nonguilty take plea deals for several reasons. The guilty sees a plea as an avenue to escape harsh punishment, but other factors render this untrue. Evidence show the minorities end up with harsher punishments with a plea in most cases. Research also show that minorities, not guilty, are cajoled into taking a plea for fear that a racially motivated jury may find them guilty. The lack of resources to hire a reputable lawyer or ignorance and naivety are reasons that individuals, while not guilty accept a guilty plea. In each of these scenarios, evidence points to minorities as being disadvantaged. This subchapter contains information about various scenarios, along with references to relevant research work in these specific areas.

Guilty Plea and disparities in bargaining

One of the most troubling aspects of the criminal justice system in America is the racial discrimination that affects the outcomes of plea bargains. Plea bargains are agreements between prosecutors and defendants in which the latter plead guilty to a lesser charge or a reduced sentence in exchange for avoiding a trial. According to some studies, plea bargains account for more than 90% of criminal convictions in the United States. However, not all defendants receive the same treatment or opportunities in the plea-bargaining process. Research has shown that there are significant racial disparities in plea deals that suggest that prosecutors may be using race as a proxy for criminality.

The study by Carlos Berdejó of Loyola Law School analyzed more than 30,000 misdemeanor cases in Wisconsin over a seven-year period and found that white defendants were 25% more likely than Black defendants to have their most serious initial charge dropped or reduced to a less severe charge (Berdejó, 2017). Black defendants were more likely than whites to be convicted of their highest initial charge. As a result, white defendants who faced initial felony charges were approximately 15% more likely than similar Black defendants to be convicted of a misdemeanor instead. White defendants with no prior convictions were over 25% more likely than Black defendants with no prior convictions to receive a charge reduction. The study concluded that disparities in plea bargaining outcomes appear to be driven by cases in which defendants have no prior conviction, which "suggests that in the absence of evidence of a defendant's recidivism risk (e.g., when there is no criminal history), prosecutors may be using race as a proxy for the defendant's likelihood to recidivate."

Similarly, a study by The Marshall Project and ProPublica examined more than 48,000 felony cases in Florida and found that white defendants were more likely than Black defendants to have their charges reduced or dropped altogether (Berdejó & Angwin, 2017). The study also found that white defendants who had an attorney were twice as likely as Black defendants who had an attorney to get such favorable outcomes. The study noted that prosecutors have wide discretion in deciding which charges to file and how to resolve them, and that they often make these decisions based on limited information and implicit biases. The study quoted one former prosecutor who said: "You are negotiating with human beings who come with all sorts of biases. And you are negotiating with facts that are given to you by human beings who come with all sorts of biases."

Furthermore, a report by Fair Trials, an international human rights organization, highlighted how plea bargaining reinforces racism within the US criminal system (Fair Trials, 2018). The report stated that Black and Latino people get worse offers than white people, and also get less counseling about making a decision to waive their right to a trial. The report cited data from New York City showing that for misdemeanor marijuana cases, Black people were 19% more likely than white people to be offered a plea deal that involves prison. The report also pointed out how plea bargaining can contribute to mass incarceration and wrongful convictions, especially for people of color who face harsher penalties and more pressure to plead guilty.

These studies and reports indicate that racial discrimination in plea bargaining is a serious problem that undermines the fairness and legitimacy of the criminal justice system. Plea bargaining is supposed to be a voluntary and rational choice for defendants who want to avoid the risks and costs of a trial. However, when race influences the offers and outcomes of plea bargains, it becomes a coercive and unjust mechanism that violates the rights and dignity of people of color.

Innocent minorities plead guilty

One of the most puzzling questions in criminal justice is why some innocent people accept plea deals instead of going to trial. Plea deals are very common in the U.S., as they allow the prosecution to avoid lengthy and costly trials and secure convictions more easily. However, they also pose a risk of wrongful convictions. One unfortunate aspects of the criminal justice system in the United States is the phenomenon of innocent people pleading guilty to crimes they did not commit. According to the

National Registry of Exonerations, 23% of exonerated defendants had previously entered a guilty plea, often under pressure from prosecutors or to avoid harsher sentences.

The incentives or coercion from the prosecution or the defense. Prosecutors may offer generous plea deals that are hard to refuse, especially if they have weak evidence or want to clear their caseloads. Defense attorneys may also encourage their clients to take plea deals, either because they believe it is in their best interest or because they want to avoid a trial that may require more work or resources.

This problem disproportionately affects Black Americans, who are seven times more likely than white Americans to be falsely convicted of serious crimes, such as murder and sexual assault (Ince, 2022). One of the reasons why Black Americans who did not commit crimes end up taking guilty pleas is the racial bias and misconduct of police officers, who are more likely to target, arrest, and coerce confessions from Black suspects (Ince, 2022). Regrettably, this also breeds fear of a harsher penalty if convicted at trial. According to the National Association of Criminal Defense Lawyers, the average sentence post-trial is triple that of the average sentence pre-trial, giving defendants a strong incentive to avoid the trial penalty.

Another reason is the difficulty of cross-racial eyewitness identification, which can lead to false accusations and convictions of Black defendants, especially in sexual assault cases (Ince, 2022). The uncertainty and stress of going to trial. Trials are unpredictable and stressful, especially for defendants who face serious charges and potential consequences. Some defendants may prefer to have some control over their outcome and avoid the risk of being wrongfully convicted by a biased jury or a faulty forensic analysis.

A third reason is the lack of adequate legal representation and resources for Black defendants, who may not have access to effective counsel, forensic experts, or DNA testing that could prove their innocence (Brown, 2023). The lack of resources or representation to mount an effective defense emanates from the fact that many defendants are indigent and rely on overworked and underfunded public defenders who may not have enough time or expertise to investigate their cases or challenge the prosecution's evidence. Indigent defendants are also more likely to be detained pre-trial, which may affect their ability to participate in their defense or maintain their employment and family ties.

These factors, among others, may create a situation where

an innocent person feels that taking a plea deal is the best option available, even if it means giving up their right to a fair trial and admitting guilt to a crime they did not commit. Sadly, these factors create a system that is stacked against Black Americans and incentivizes them to accept plea bargains that spare them from the risk of harsher penalties, such as life imprisonment or death penalty, but also deprive them of their constitutional rights and dignity. This has serious implications for the integrity and legitimacy of the criminal justice system, as it undermines the presumption of innocence and the right to due process. Moreover, it may result in wrongful convictions that harm not only the innocent defendants, but also the victims, the public, and the rule of law.

HISTORY OF RACIALLY MOTIVATED CREDIT DISCRIMINATION

Credit discrimination is the practice of denying or limiting access to credit based on factors other than a borrower's creditworthiness, such as race, color, religion, national origin, sex, marital status, age, or source of income. Credit discrimination has a long and shameful history in the United States, and it has contributed to the racial wealth gap and economic inequality that persist today. Some of the historical examples of credit discrimination include:

Redlining

This was the systematic denial of mortgages and other loans to residents of certain neighborhoods, mostly Black and minority communities, based on their racial composition. Redlining was facilitated by the federal Homeowners' Loan Corporation (HOLC), which created color-coded maps that graded areas by their perceived credit risk. Red areas were considered hazardous and ineligible for federal backing, while green areas were considered desirable and safe. Redlining effectively shut out Black and minority borrowers from homeownership and wealth accumulation, while subsidizing white suburbanization. Redlining was outlawed by the Fair Housing Act of 1968, but its effects are still visible today in the patterns of residential segregation, disinvestment, and poverty (SpringerLink, 2022).

Redlining was not only a federal policy, but also a widespread practice among private lenders, such as banks and thrifts. Lenders often relied on the FHA's maps and guidelines to determine their own lending policies or used their own criteria to exclude Black borrowers or charge them higher interest rates and fees. Private lenders were regulated by agencies such as the Federal Reserve, which had the authority to examine their lending practices and ensure their safety and soundness. However, there is little evidence that the Federal Reserve or other regulators challenged or intervened in the redlining practices of private lenders before the 1960s. Instead, they focused on limiting the amount and duration of mortgage loans that banks could make, fearing that they would jeopardize their liquidity and solvency (Federal Reserve History, 2023).

    The civil rights movement of the 1950s and 1960s challenged the legal and social foundations of racial discrimination in various aspects of American life, including credit. The Fair Housing Act of 1968 was a landmark legislation that prohibited discrimination in the sale, rental, or financing of housing based on race, color, religion, sex, or national origin. The Fair Housing Act also assigned federal financial regulators, including the Federal Reserve, the responsibility of enforcing its provisions and preventing redlining. In the following decades, regulators took several steps to implement the Fair Housing Act, such as issuing guidelines for fair lending practices, conducting examinations and investigations of lenders' compliance, and imposing sanctions for violations. The Fair Housing Act was also supplemented by other laws that aimed to promote equal access to credit, such as the Equal Credit Opportunity Act of 1974, the Home Mortgage Disclosure Act of 1975, and the Community Reinvestment Act of 1977 (Federal Reserve History, 2023).

Racially restrictive covenants

These were clauses in property deeds that prohibited the sale or rental of a property to people of certain races, ethnicities, or religions. Racially restrictive covenants were widely used in the early 20th century to maintain white-only neighborhoods and exclude Black and minority families from certain areas. Racially restrictive covenants were declared unenforceable by the U.S. Supreme Court in 1948, but they remained in some deeds until the Fair Housing Act banned them.

Predatory lending

This is the practice of offering loans with unfair or abusive terms and conditions, such as high interest rates, excessive fees, hidden charges, or prepayment penalties. Predatory lending targets vulnerable borrowers who have limited access to conventional credit sources, such as low-income, elderly, or minority consumers. Predatory lending can trap borrowers in cycles of debt and strip them of their assets and equity. Predatory lending can take various forms, such as payday loans, auto title loans, subprime mortgages, or rent-to-own contracts.

To combat credit discrimination, several federal laws have been enacted to protect borrowers' rights and ensure fair access to credit, such as the Equal Credit Opportunity Act of 1974, the Community Reinvestment Act of 1977, and the Dodd-Frank Wall Street Reform and Consumer Protection Act of 2010. However, more work is needed to enforce these laws, monitor credit practices, educate consumers, and promote financial inclusion and empowerment for all.

Despite these legal and regulatory efforts, racial discrimination in credit has not been eliminated. Studies have shown that Black borrowers still face disparities in access to credit, terms of credit, and outcomes of credit compared to white borrowers. These disparities can be attributed to various factors, such as differences in income, wealth, education, credit history, and neighborhood characteristics. However, some studies have also found evidence of discrimination based on race alone, such as differential treatment by loan officers or brokers, steering into subprime or predatory loans, or denial or pricing based on racial proxies or stereotypes. These forms of discrimination can have significant negative effects on Black borrowers' financial well-being and economic opportunities (SpringerLink, 2022).

These are just some of the ways that credit discrimination has harmed Black and minority borrowers in the past and present. Credit discrimination not only violates the principles of equal opportunity and justice, but also undermines the economic potential and stability of individuals and communities.

RACIAL DISCRIMINATION IN CREDIT AND TAXES

The Equal Credit Opportunity Act (ECOA) is a federal law that was enacted in 1974 to protect consumers from discrimination in credit transactions. The ECOA prohibits creditors from denying or limiting credit to any applicant based on factors other than their creditworthiness, such as race, color, religion, national origin, sex, marital status, age, source of income, or exercise of rights under the Consumer Credit Protection Act. The ECOA applies to any person or entity that regularly extends, renews, or participates in credit decisions, such as banks, credit unions, credit card companies, mortgage lenders, retailers, and finance companies.

The ECOA aims to ensure fair and equal access to credit for all Americans and to promote economic opportunity and justice. The ECOA also requires creditors to provide applicants with the reasons for any adverse action taken on their credit applications, such as denial, higher interest rate, or lower credit limit. Additionally, the ECOA mandates that creditors provide applicants with a copy of all appraisals and other written valuations used in connection with their applications for first lien loans secured by a dwelling.

The ECOA is enforced by several federal agencies, depending on the type of creditor involved. For example, the Federal Trade Commission (FTC) enforces the ECOA for most non-bank creditors, while the Consumer Financial Protection Bureau (CFPB) enforces the ECOA for banks, credit unions, and other financial institutions. The Department of Justice (DOJ) also has authority to bring lawsuits against creditors for violations of the ECOA. Consumers who believe they have been discriminated against by a creditor can file a complaint with the appropriate federal agency or sue the creditor in court. The remedies available under the ECOA include actual damages, punitive damages, injunctive relief, and attorney's fees.

Despite the ECOA, it is a well-known fact that Black people in America pay more for credits than their white counterparts, even when controlling for factors such as income, education and credit history. This racial disparity in credit costs has significant implications for the economic well-being and mobility of Black Americans, who face higher interest rates, fees and debt burdens than whites. According to various studies, some of the sources of this disparity include:

Mortgage market discrimination

Black borrowers are less likely to get approved for mortgages, and when they do, they pay higher interest rates and fees than white borrowers with similar credit profiles. A University of California Berkeley study found that Black mortgage borrowers pay an average of 0.08% more in interest than white borrowers with comparable credit, which costs borrowers over $760 million more every year.

Student loan debt

Black students are more likely to take on student loans, and more of them, than white students, due to lower levels of family wealth and financial aid. They also face higher default rates and lower repayment rates than white students, partly because of lower earnings and higher unemployment after graduation. Black adults (50%) were more likely than white adults (44%) and Hispanic/Latino adults (37%) to have student debt. The same patterns appeared with average debt levels; women ($9,400) had higher student debt levels than men ($7,700), and Black adults ($9,800) had more student debt than white adults ($8,700) and Hispanic/Latino adults ($7,000).

High-interest debt

Black households are more likely to use high-cost forms of credit, such as payday loans, auto title loans, pawn shops and rent-to-own stores, than white households. These alternative financial services often charge exorbitant fees and interest rates, trapping borrowers in cycles of debt. However, because blacks owed larger amounts of high-interest debt—such as installment credit and student and car loans—the debt they typically owed was more expensive. For example, blacks carry larger credit card balances than whites.

In addition to these structural factors, many blacks also avoid seeking credit due to generations of discrimination and mistreatment by the federal government and financial institutions. This results in a lack of credit history or low credit scores, which further reduces their chances of obtaining affordable credit products. According to the Consumer Financial Protection Bureau, roughly 15% of black consumers are considered credit invisible, meaning they do not have enough credit history to generate a score, compared with 9% among white consumers. An additional 13% of black consumers have unscored records, meaning they have insufficient or outdated information in their credit reports. These numbers indicate that many Black people are either excluded from or disadvantaged by the mainstream credit system.

These examples illustrate how systemic racism and inequality affect the credit market and the financial opportunities of Black Americans. It is clear that race plays a significant role in shaping the credit outcomes of black Americans. Reducing the racial gap in credit costs requires addressing the root causes of discrimination and disadvantage that limit the access and affordability of credit for Black Americans. To address this issue, it is necessary to challenge the discriminatory practices and policies that create and maintain racial disparities in credit access and cost. It is also important to empower black consumers with financial education and counseling, as well as alternative credit scoring models that can capture their creditworthiness more accurately and fairly.

Black tax

The Black Tax is a term that describes the financial costs of discrimination against Black Americans. It refers to the higher prices and interest rates that Black Americans pay for goods and services, such as cars, mortgages, and credit cards, compared to white Americans with similar income and credit profiles. It also refers to the lower wages, wealth, and opportunities that Black Americans face due to historical and ongoing racism and oppression. The Black Tax reduces the economic power and potential of Black Americans and contributes to the racial wealth gap that exists in the United States. Here are some examples of how the Black Tax affects different aspects of life:

Education

Black students often face higher tuition fees, lower financial aid, and more student debt than white students. According to a 2019 report by the Center for American Progress, Black students borrow more than white students at every degree level and are more likely to default on their loans.

The severity of Black tax on the education of Black people

One of the areas where the Black Tax has a significant impact is education. Black students face many challenges and disadvantages in accessing and completing quality education, such as:

- Lower funding and resources for schools that serve predominantly Black students, resulting in less qualified teachers, outdated textbooks, and inadequate facilities.

- Higher tuition fees and lower financial aid for college, resulting in more student debt and lower graduation rates for Black students.

- Lower expectations and biases from teachers and counselors, resulting in less academic support and guidance for

Black students.

- Less access to advanced courses, extracurricular activities, and enrichment programs that prepare students for college and careers.

- More exposure to disciplinary actions, such as suspensions and expulsions, which disrupt learning and increase the risk of dropping out.

The UNCF reports that Black children are less likely than white children to be ready for college, as 61% of the Black high school students who took the ACT in 2015 met none of the four ACT college readiness benchmarks. That is almost twice the rate of all students who took the ACT that year. Even when they do attend college, they face higher student debt and lower earnings than their white peers. The Education Trust states that Black students borrow more than white students to pay for college, and they are more likely to default on their loans due to lower incomes and higher unemployment rates.

The Black tax also has a psychological dimension, as Black people experience stress and anxiety from thinking about how white Americans perceive their social construct of blackness. Blackness in America is often portrayed through a deficit lens and is associated with racial stereotypes that affect their self-esteem and performance. A study by Diverse Education proposes a concept of the Black tax to understand the experiences of Black people in America and suggests that educators should be aware of this phenomenon and provide culturally responsive pedagogy and support for Black students.

These challenges limit the educational opportunities and outcomes for Black students and create barriers to their economic and social mobility. The Black Tax on education not only affects individual students, but also their families and communities, who may rely on them for financial support. To reduce the Black Tax on education, policy makers and educators need to address the systemic racism and inequality that affect the quality and affordability of education for Black students.

Employment

Black workers often face lower wages, fewer promotions, and more discrimination than white workers. According to a 2020 report by McKinsey & Company, Black workers are underrepresented in high-paying occupations and overrepresented in low-paying ones. The report also found that the median hourly wage for Black workers is 21% lower than that of white workers.

Housing

Black homeowners often pay more for mortgages, insurance, and property taxes than white homeowners. According to a 2020 study by MIT researchers, Black homeowners pay an average of 13% more in annual property taxes than white homeowners with similar properties. The study also found that Black homeowners pay higher interest rates and mortgage insurance premiums than white homeowners with similar credit scores.

Business

Black entrepreneurs often face more barriers and challenges than white entrepreneurs. According to a 2020 report by the Brookings Institution, Black-owned businesses receive less funding, have lower revenues, and are more likely to fail than white-owned businesses. The report also found that Black-owned businesses are less likely to receive loans from banks and more likely to rely on personal savings or credit cards.

The Curtain That Divides US: A metaphor for society's Perpetual Inequalities.
Message for the youths

EDUCATIONAL INEQUALITY: ACCESS AND QUALITY

Education is widely recognized as a crucial tool for personal and societal development. It has the power to transform lives, break the cycle of poverty, and empower individuals to reach their full potential. However, educational inequality remains a persistent challenge that hampers progress and perpetuates social divisions. In this subchapter, we will delve into the issues of access and quality in education, and biases leading to discrimination and unmerited disciplinary actions against Black students. All these shedding light on the enduring inequalities that hinder our collective advancement.

Access to education is the first hurdle that many individuals face. Across the globe, there are still millions of children and adults who are denied the right to education due to various barriers such as poverty, gender discrimination, disability, and conflict. This denial of education not only robs individuals of their potential but also hampers societal progress. It is imperative that we address this disparity and work towards ensuring that every person, regardless of their background or circumstances, has equal access to quality education.

Moreover, even when access is granted, the quality of

education provided often varies greatly. Educational institutions in marginalized communities are often underfunded, lacking proper resources, trained teachers, and infrastructure.

A number of studies have shown that Black students face disproportionate and unfair disciplinary actions in schools compared to their white peers. For instance, the American Psychological Association reported that Black students were more likely to be suspended for minor offenses than white students, which can have detrimental effects on their academic achievement and school climate. Similarly, the U.S. Government Accountability Office found that Black students, boys, and students with disabilities were overrepresented in discipline rates, mainly suspensions and expulsions, in K-12 public schools during the 2013-2014 school year (American Psychological Association, 2021 & GAO, 2018).

"Unfortunately, we were not surprised by the findings, considering what we know about the role of racial bias in painting school adults' views of African American youth as less innocent, older and more aggressive than their white peers. Regardless of the behavior that African American youth engage in, that behavior is viewed by educators as more worthy of harsh school discipline like a suspension," (Ming-te Wang, 2021).

This leads to a subpar learning experience and perpetuates the cycle of inequality. We must advocate for equitable distribution of resources, invest in teacher training and support, and create an environment that fosters a love for learning.

The enduring inequalities in society, symbolized by the metaphorical "curtain," are deeply interconnected with educational inequality. The curtain that divides us represents not only the physical barriers but also the social, economic, and cultural divisions. Addressing educational inequality is crucial for dismantling this curtain and creating a more equitable society. It is the responsibility of all ages, from the youngest to the oldest, to recognize these inequalities and actively work towards their eradication.

To the youths, we convey a message of empowerment and hope. You possess the energy, enthusiasm, and determination needed to challenge the status quo and spearhead change. By raising your voice, advocating for equal educational opportunities, and supporting initiatives that strive for educational equity, you can contribute to breaking down the curtain and creating a fairer world for all.

Educational inequality continues to hinder progress and perpetuate social divisions. Access to education remains a challenge for many, and the quality of education provided varies greatly.

These factors are further exacerbated by the discriminatory disciplinary tendencies against Black students. Addressing these issues requires a collective effort from all ages and a commitment to dismantling the enduring inequalities in society. By empowering ourselves with knowledge, advocating for change, and supporting initiatives that promote educational equity, we can rise above the curtain and create a more inclusive and just world.

THE INVISIBLE BARRIERS OF CLASS

In a world that prides itself on progress and equality, it is disheartening to acknowledge the enduring inequalities that persist in our society. Despite the advancements we have made in technology, education, and social justice, there remains an invisible barrier that divides us – the barrier of class.

Class has long been a divisive force, determining access to resources, opportunities, and even basic human rights. It is a system that categorizes individuals based on their wealth, education, and social status, perpetuating a cycle of privilege and disadvantage. This invisible barrier not only divides us but also limits the potential of countless individuals, particularly those from marginalized communities.

The Curtain That Divides US: A metaphor for society's Perpetual Inequalities.
Message for the youths

The consequences of this invisible barrier are far-reaching, impacting every aspect of our lives. From education to healthcare, housing to employment, class influences the opportunities available to us. The privileged or those born into wealth often have access to the best schools, healthcare, and job prospects, while those from lower-class backgrounds face limited options and systemic hurdles that prevent them from breaking free from the cycle of poverty.

For the youths of today, understanding and confronting these invisible barriers of class is crucial. They hold the power to challenge the status quo and reshape our society for the better. By raising awareness, advocating for equal opportunities, and working towards dismantling the invisible barriers, they can pave the way for a more just and equitable future.

Breaking down these barriers requires not only collective action but also empathy and understanding. We must recognize that class is not a reflection of an individual's worth or abilities, but rather a product of a deeply flawed system. By fostering empathy, we can bridge the gap between different classes and work towards a society where everyone has access to the same opportunities, regardless of their background.

This subchapter serves as a call to action for all ages. It is a reminder that the invisible barriers of class are not insurmountable, but they require our collective efforts to dismantle them. It is a message for the youths, who hold the power to shape the future, to rise above these barriers and fight for a more inclusive and equal society.

Let us come together, across generations, and work towards a world where the curtain that divides us based on class is torn down. Only then can we truly empower all individuals, giving them the chance to rise above their circumstances and achieve their fullest potential.

THE EFFECTS OF SEGREGATION AND GENTRIFICATION

In our modern society, the issues of segregation and gentrification continue to plague our communities, creating a stark divide among different social groups. These phenomena, rooted in historical and systemic inequalities, have significant and lasting effects on individuals, families, and entire communities. It is crucial for people of all ages to understand and address these issues in order to fight against inequality and build a more inclusive society.

Segregation, the separation of people based on race,

ethnicity, or socioeconomic status, perpetuates a cycle of inequality by limiting access to resources and opportunities. When communities are segregated, certain groups are systematically disadvantaged, facing limited access to quality education, healthcare, employment opportunities, and safe neighborhoods. This creates a stark contrast between privileged and marginalized communities, further widening the gap between them.

The consequences of segregation are far-reaching and affect individuals throughout their lives. Children growing up in segregated neighborhoods often attend underfunded schools with fewer resources and less experienced teachers. This educational disadvantage hinders their chances of success later in life, perpetuating a cycle of poverty. Additionally, living in segregated communities can lead to increased crime rates, limited access to healthcare, and reduced social mobility, trapping individuals in a cycle of disadvantage that is difficult to escape.

Gentrification, on the other hand, occurs when wealthier individuals and businesses move into historically marginalized neighborhoods, leading to rising property values and the displacement of long-term residents. While gentrification may bring some benefits, such as increased investment and improved infrastructure, it often results in the displacement of low-income residents who can no longer afford the rising costs of living. This uprooting of communities erodes social ties and disrupts the support networks that residents rely on.

For all ages, it is essential to recognize the negative consequences of segregation and gentrification and actively work towards dismantling these systems. By understanding the root causes of these issues, we can advocate for equitable policies that promote integration, affordable housing, and equal access to resources. Engaging in community organizing, volunteering, and supporting organizations that fight for social justice can also make a significant impact.

To the younger generation, who will shape the future of our society, it is crucial to understand the enduring inequalities that exist and be the catalysts for change. By educating themselves, engaging in dialogue, and challenging the status quo, they can ensure a more equitable future for all. It is within their power to break down the curtain that divides us and create a society where everyone has an equal opportunity to thrive.

The effects of segregation and gentrification have far-reaching consequences on individuals and communities. By recognizing these issues and actively working towards a more inclusive society, people of all ages can fight against inequality and ensure a brighter future for all. Together, we can rise above the curtain that separates us and empower generations to come.

THE ROLE OF GENDER AND INTERSECTIONALITY

In today's society, it is crucial to understand the role of gender and intersectionality in order to dismantle the enduring inequalities that persist within our communities. Gender, as a social construct, plays a significant role in shaping individual experiences and opportunities, often leading to disparities between men and women. However, it is equally important to recognize how intersecting identities, such as race, class, sexuality, and ability, further complicate these dynamics.

Gender inequality affects individuals of all ages, from young children to the elderly. It permeates every aspect of our lives, including education, employment, healthcare, and even personal relationships. By recognizing and challenging these gendered norms, we can empower individuals to rise above the curtain of inequality.

The Curtain That Divides US: A metaphor for society's Perpetual Inequalities.
Message for the youths

One of the key aspects of understanding gender is acknowledging its intersectionality. Intersectionality recognizes that individuals embody multiple social identities that interact with and influence one another. For example, a woman's experience of gender inequality may be further compounded if she also belongs to a marginalized racial or ethnic group. Intersectionality reminds us that inequalities are not experienced in isolation but are interconnected and mutually reinforcing.

By addressing the role of gender and intersectionality, we can shed light on the unique challenges faced by different individuals and communities. This understanding allows us to develop more inclusive and equitable solutions that cater to the needs of all. For example, in education, we can examine how gender biases influence educational outcomes and work towards creating an environment that fosters equal opportunities for all genders. In the workplace, we can strive to eradicate gender-based discrimination, ensuring fair hiring practices, equal pay, and opportunities for career advancement.

Moreover, it is crucial to involve the youth in these discussions. By empowering young individuals with knowledge about gender and intersectionality, we can foster a generation that challenges and dismantles inequalities. Educating the youth about the importance of inclusive language, empathy, and respect can cultivate a society that values diversity and equality.

The role of gender and intersectionality cannot be overlooked when addressing enduring inequalities in society. Understanding the complexities of these concepts allows us to develop strategies and solutions that promote fairness and inclusivity for all ages. By working together, we can rise above the curtain of inequality and create a more equitable and just world for everyone.

THE CURTAIN OF INEQUALITY: HOW IT DIVIDES US

In today's society, there is a curtain that divides us, a curtain woven from the threads of inequality. This curtain casts a shadow over our lives, dividing us into haves and have-nots, creating an uneven playing field where opportunities are limited, and dreams seem out of reach. It is a barrier that affects people of all ages, from the very young to the elderly, and it is time for us to rise above it.

The curtain of inequality is not a new phenomenon; it has been present throughout history. However, in our modern world, it

The Curtain That Divides US: A metaphor for society's Perpetual Inequalities.
Message for the youths

manifests itself in various forms, be it economic, social, or educational disparities. It is a curtain that separates us based on our race, gender, socioeconomic status, and more. It is a silent divider that perpetuates injustice and fuels the flames of discontentment and unrest in our society.

For the youth, this curtain of inequality can be particularly disheartening. They are the ones who will inherit the world we leave behind, and yet, they face immense challenges and obstacles due to this curtain. Many young people are denied access to quality education, healthcare, and equal opportunities for success. They are told that their dreams are unattainable simply because of the circumstances they were born into.

But we must not allow this curtain to define us. We must rise above it, empowering ourselves and others to fight against the injustices it represents. We must recognize that we are all connected, and the inequalities faced by one person affect us all. By uniting and working together, we can tear down this curtain, creating a more just and equitable society.

To the young generation, we say: Do not be discouraged by the challenges that lie before you. Instead, let them fuel your determination to create a better world. Use your voices to speak out against inequality, demand change, and inspire others to join the fight. Remember, you are the architects of the future, and it is in your hands to dismantle this curtain of inequality and build a more inclusive and compassionate society.

To people of all ages, we urge you to educate yourselves about the various forms of inequality that exist in our world. Understand that this curtain affects us all, directly, or indirectly. It is only by acknowledging and addressing these inequalities that we can hope to create a more harmonious and just society.

The curtain of inequality is a pervasive force that divides us, but it is not insurmountable. By working together, across all ages and backgrounds, we can rise above it and create a world where everyone has equal opportunities to thrive. Let us empower ourselves and others to fight against injustice, tearing down the curtain that divides us and embracing a future where equality reigns supreme.

CHAPTER 2: EMPOWERING THE YOUTH TO BREAK THE CURTAIN

HOW YOUTHS CAN COMBAT SOCIETIES INEQUALITIES

Youths are the future of society, and they have the potential to make positive changes in the world. However, they also face many challenges and barriers due to various forms of inequality, such as racial discrimination, gender bias, economic disparity, and social exclusion. How can youths combat these inequalities and create a more just and inclusive society for themselves and others?

One way is to listen and educate themselves about the experiences and perspectives of people who face racism, sexism, xenophobia, and other forms of oppression every day. By paying attention to the voices of friends, classmates, neighbors, and community leaders who belong to different races, ethnicities, genders, sexual orientations, and backgrounds, youths can learn about the causes and consequences of inequality, as well as the ways to challenge stereotypes and prejudices (UNICEF, 2020).

Another way is to raise awareness about the issues of

inequality and injustice in their communities and beyond. Youths can use various platforms and tools, such as social media, blogs, podcasts, art, music, and sports, to share their opinions, stories, and solutions with others. They can also join or organize campaigns, movements, and events that advocate for human rights, social justice, and environmental sustainability (Price-Mitchell, 2022).

A third way is to challenge everyday discrimination and racism that they encounter or witness in their schools, workplaces, public spaces, or online. Youths can speak up against hateful or harmful comments or actions that target people based on their identity or appearance. They can also report racist or discriminatory content online to the relevant authorities or platforms (UN, 2021).

A fourth way is to support and collaborate with other youths who are working to combat inequality in different ways. Youths can join or form groups, clubs, networks, or organizations that focus on specific issues or goals related to equality and inclusion. They can also participate in local or global initiatives that connect youths from diverse backgrounds and cultures to exchange ideas, experiences, and resources (Flores & Pinkerton, 2021).

A fifth way is to demand that their schools or universities take action against racism and discrimination in their policies and practices. Youths can ask for more inclusive curricula that reflect the diversity of human history and culture. They can also request more opportunities for intercultural dialogue and learning among students and staff. They can also urge their institutions to adopt anti-racist and anti-discriminatory measures that protect the rights and dignity of all members of the academic community (Lemerise 2016).

These are some of the ways that youths can combat society's inequalities. By taking these actions, youths can not only improve their own lives but also contribute to the common good of humanity.

THE POWER OF EDUCATION: A TOOL FOR EQUALITY

In the journey towards a more equal and just society, education stands tall as a powerful tool that can break down the barriers of inequality. Regardless of age, education has the potential to empower individuals and transform communities. This subchapter delves into the profound impact of education and its ability to bridge the gap caused by enduring inequalities in our society.

The Curtain That Divides US: A metaphor for society's Perpetual Inequalities.
Message for the youths

Education is the key that unlocks the doors to opportunity, enabling individuals to rise above the curtain of inequality. It equips people with knowledge, skills, and critical thinking abilities, empowering them to challenge societal norms and pursue their dreams. Through education, individuals can acquire the tools necessary to advocate for equality and fight against the injustices that persist in our world.

For the youth, education is a beacon of hope. It provides them with the means to overcome adversity and create a better future. By investing in their education, we invest in the next generation of leaders, change-makers, and equality advocates. Education empowers young people to challenge the status quo, question societal norms, and strive for a more inclusive society. It enables them to rise above the curtain and break free from the limitations imposed by inequality.

However, the power of education extends far beyond the young generation. Education knows no age limits and can be a transformative force for individuals of all ages. It has the potential to empower adults, giving them the tools to reshape their lives and break free from the cycle of inequality. By embracing lifelong learning, individuals can acquire new skills, broaden their perspectives, and enhance their employability, thereby increasing their chances of achieving economic and social equality.

Moreover, education fosters empathy and understanding, promoting a more inclusive society. It enables individuals to gain insight into the experiences and struggles faced by marginalized groups, fostering a sense of compassion and a desire for change. By educating ourselves and others, we can break down the curtain that separates us and work towards a society that celebrates diversity and equality.

In conclusion, education is a powerful tool for equality that has the potential to transform lives and communities. It empowers individuals of all ages to rise above the curtain of inequality, challenge societal norms, and fight for a more just and inclusive world. By investing in education, we invest in the future of our society, equipping individuals with the knowledge and skills necessary to create lasting change. Let us embrace the power of education and work together to dismantle the enduring inequalities that plague our society.

The Curtain That Divides US: A metaphor for society's Perpetual Inequalities.
Message for the youths

IMPROVING ACCESS TO QUALITY EDUCATION

Quality education unlocks better prospects and a brighter future. Education is a powerful tool that empowers individuals of all ages to break free from the chains of inequality and achieve their full potential. However, in many societies, there is a curtain that separates us, creating enduring inequalities in access to quality education. This subchapter aims to shed light on this issue and provide a message for the youths, who hold the power to dismantle this curtain and create a more equitable society.

In today's world, education is not a privilege but a fundamental right that should be accessible to all. Unfortunately, numerous barriers prevent many individuals, especially those from marginalized communities, from accessing quality education. These barriers result in all sorts of constraints including financial constraints, lack of infrastructure, inadequate resources, and discriminatory practices. It is imperative that we address these challenges and work towards creating an inclusive education system that leaves no one behind.

To improve access to quality education, we must first recognize the importance of investing in education at all levels. Governments, civil society organizations, and individuals must prioritize education and allocate adequate resources to ensure that every child has the opportunity to go to school. This includes providing scholarships, building schools in remote areas, and implementing policies that promote inclusivity and diversity in the education system.

Furthermore, technology can play a crucial role in bridging the gap in access to education. Online platforms, virtual classrooms, and e-learning tools can provide opportunities for individuals who may not have access to traditional educational institutions. By harnessing the power of technology, we can create a more inclusive and flexible learning environment that caters to the diverse needs of learners.

However, improving access to education is not enough. We must also focus on the quality of education being provided. It is essential to invest in teacher training and ensure that educators have the necessary tools and support to deliver high-quality education. Additionally, curricula should be updated to reflect the changing needs of society, and students should be equipped with the skills required to thrive in the 21st- century job market.

To the youths, you hold the power to bring about change and tear down the curtain of inequality in education. Your voices are powerful, and your actions can make a difference. Advocate for equal access to education, raise awareness about the importance of quality education, and support initiatives that aim to improve educational opportunities for all. Remember, education is not just a personal asset; it is a catalyst for social change and a means to build a better, more inclusive world.

In conclusion, improving access to quality education is vital for combating inequality and empowering individuals of all ages. By investing in education, leveraging technology, and focusing on quality, we can break down the curtain that separates us and create a more equitable society. The youths have the power to make a difference. Let us join hands and rise above the curtain, empowering all ages to fight inequality through education.

ADDRESSING EDUCATIONAL DISPARITIES

Education is often hailed as the great equalizer, the tool that can bridge the gap between the haves and the have-nots. However, the reality is that educational disparities persist, creating a curtain that divides individuals and perpetuates enduring inequalities in society. In this subchapter, we delve into the importance of addressing these disparities and empowering all ages to fight against inequality.

Educational disparities are multi-faceted, encompassing various factors such as socio- economic status, race, gender, and geographic location. These disparities manifest in unequal access to quality education, resources, and opportunities. The consequences are far-reaching, with disadvantaged individuals facing limited career prospects, reduced social mobility, and a perpetuation of the cycle of poverty.

To dismantle this curtain of inequality, it is crucial to recognize that addressing educational disparities is not solely the responsibility of educational institutions or policymakers. Each one of us has a role to play in empowering all ages and creating a more equitable society.

For young people, understanding the realities of educational disparities is essential. By recognizing the privilege they may have, they can develop empathy and a sense of social responsibility. They can actively engage in initiatives that support marginalized communities, such as tutoring programs, mentorship, or advocating for policy changes that promote equal educational opportunities.

Adults also have a crucial role to play. Parents and guardians can advocate for their children, ensuring they have access to quality education regardless of skin tone or their background. They can actively participate in school boards and parent-teacher associations, demanding equitable resource allocation and supportive learning environments.

Additionally, adults can engage in lifelong learning themselves, setting an example for younger generations and reinforcing the importance of education.

Educational institutions must also take significant strides to address these disparities. They should adopt inclusive policies that promote diversity and eliminate discriminatory practices. Investing in teacher training programs that foster cultural sensitivity and equitable teaching practices is essential. Furthermore, schools should develop comprehensive support systems, including access to mental health services, tutoring, and college guidance, to ensure that all students can thrive.

To truly rise above the curtain of educational disparities, we must foster collaboration between all stakeholders. Government agencies, non-profit organizations, and private entities should work together to allocate resources and design programs that target the most vulnerable communities. By pooling our efforts, we can create a society where every individual, regardless of skin color or their background, has an equal opportunity to succeed.

In conclusion, addressing educational disparities is a collective responsibility that requires the engagement of all ages. By raising awareness, fostering empathy, and taking action, we can empower individuals to fight inequality and create a more equitable society. Let us join hands, rise above the curtain, and ensure that education becomes the powerful tool it is meant to be – one that opens doors and eliminates barriers for all.

ENCOURAGING LIFELONG LEARNING

In the pursuit of a fair and equitable society, one of the most powerful tools we have is lifelong learning. Regardless of age or background, the quest for knowledge and personal growth should never cease. Lifelong learning is the key that unlocks doors to new opportunities and empowers individuals to rise above the curtain of inequality that separates us.

For the youths, this message is particularly crucial. In today's fast-paced and ever- evolving world, the ability to adapt and learn continuously is more important than ever before. By embracing lifelong learning, young people can equip themselves with the skills and knowledge needed to navigate the challenges they may encounter in the future.

But the call to encourage lifelong learning extends far beyond the boundaries of youth. It applies to individuals of all ages, as it is never too late to embark on a journey of self-improvement and personal growth. Lifelong learning is a mindset that enables us to stay relevant in a rapidly changing world, to remain intellectually curious, and to continuously expand our horizons.

Furthermore, lifelong learning has the power to break down the enduring inequalities in society. By providing equal access to educational resources and opportunities, we can level the playing field and ensure that everyone has a fair chance to succeed.

Encouraging lifelong learning among all ages helps to bridge the gap between the privileged and the marginalized, fostering a more inclusive and just society.

To embrace lifelong learning, we must create an environment that nurtures curiosity and a thirst for knowledge. This can be achieved through accessible educational programs, community-based initiatives, and the integration of technology into learning platforms. By removing barriers to education and making it engaging and interactive, we can inspire individuals of all ages to embark on a lifelong learning journey.

Moreover, lifelong learning should not be limited to the traditional classroom setting. We must recognize that learning can happen in various forms and settings, such as through mentorship, experiential learning, and self-directed exploration. By promoting a holistic approach to lifelong learning, we encourage individuals to seek knowledge from diverse sources and embrace different perspectives.

In conclusion, encouraging lifelong learning is essential for individuals of all ages. It empowers the youth to overcome the enduring inequalities in society and equips them with the necessary tools to succeed. For individuals at any stage of life, embracing lifelong learning ensures personal growth, adaptability, and a more inclusive society. Let us break down the barriers that separate us and rise above the curtain of inequality through a lifelong commitment to learning and self-improvement.

YOUTH ACTIVISM: AMPLIFYING VOICES FOR CHANGE

In a world plagued by enduring inequalities, it is the youth who possess the power to dismantle the barriers that divide us.

Here, we review the remarkable impact of young activists in fighting inequality. It seeks to inspire individuals of all ages, highlighting the importance of youth engagement and the tremendous potential for change when their voices are amplified.

The Power of Young Voices

Throughout history, young people have played a pivotal role in challenging societal norms and demanding change. From the Civil Rights Movement to the fight against climate change, youth activists have brought critical issues to the forefront, forcing adults and policymakers to listen. Their passion, fearlessness, and unwavering dedication have ignited movements that have transformed societies.

Addressing Enduring Inequalities

The curtain that divides us represents the enduring inequalities that persist in our society. Whether it is racial discrimination, gender inequality, or economic disparity, these barriers hinder progress and perpetuate injustice. The message for the youth is clear: it is their responsibility to tear down this curtain and work towards a more equitable future.

Amplifying Youth Voices

In recent years, social media platforms have become powerful tools for youth activists to amplify their voices and mobilize communities. Through hashtags, viral campaigns, and online organizing, young activists have harnessed the power of technology to reach a wider audience and effect change on a global scale. They have proven that age is not a limitation but rather an advantage in the fight against inequality.

Inspiring Action

To inspire action, this subchapter features stories of remarkable young activists who have defied the odds and made a lasting impact. Their stories reminds us that anyone, regardless of age, can contribute to the fight against inequality. From Malala Yousafzai's advocacy for girls' education to Greta Thunberg's relentless fight for climate justice, these young change-makers demonstrate the power of determination and resilience.

Harnessing Collective Efforts

To truly overcome enduring inequalities, it is crucial for

individuals of all ages to come together and support youth-led movements. This subchapter encourages readers to actively engage with youth activists, whether by participating in marches, signing petitions, or supporting their initiatives financially. By harnessing our collective efforts, we can create a society that is fair, just, and inclusive for all.

Conclusion

"Youth Activism: Amplifying Voices for Change" is a call to action for individuals of all ages. It urges us to recognize the immense power and potential of young activists in the fight against enduring inequalities. By amplifying their voices, supporting their initiatives, and working together, we can tear down the curtain that separates us and build a more equitable future for all.

THE IMPORTANCE OF YOUTH ACTIVISM IN HISTORY

In the grand tapestry of history, youth activism has played an indispensable role in shaping societies and steering them towards progress. From the civil rights movements to environmental campaigns, young individuals have time and again proven their ability to challenge the status quo, ignite change, and leave an indelible mark on the world.

This subchapter aims to explore the significance of youth activism throughout history, shedding light on the transformative power it holds and the lessons it imparts to all ages.

Throughout history, young people have been at the forefront of movements fighting against enduring inequalities that pervade our societies. Their passion, energy, and unwavering belief in justice have propelled them to stand up against oppression, discrimination, and injustice. The civil rights movement of the 1960s in the United States serves as a prime example, with young activists like Martin Luther King Jr., Rosa Parks, and countless others leading the charge for racial equality. Their bravery and determination not only transformed the course of history but also inspired generations to come.

Youth activism has also been instrumental in addressing pressing environmental issues. From Greta Thunberg's global climate strikes to the Indigenous-led protests against oil pipelines, young activists have recognized the urgent need to protect our planet and have mobilized their peers and communities to take action. Their commitment to sustainable practices, renewable energy, and conservation has brought environmental concerns to the forefront of public discourse and policy agendas.

Moreover, youth activism serves as a powerful catalyst for intergenerational dialogue and collaboration. It bridges the gap between generations, demolishing the curtain that separates us and fostering understanding, empathy, and solidarity. By championing their causes, young activists inspire adults to challenge their own beliefs and biases, and together, work towards a more inclusive and equitable society.

The lessons derived from youth activism are not limited to the young alone. It teaches us all the importance of resilience, determination, and the belief in the power of our voices. It demonstrates that age is not a barrier to making a difference and that collective action can bring about real change. By empowering young people to engage in activism, we empower them to become active citizens, critical thinkers, and advocates for justice.

In conclusion, the importance of youth activism in history cannot be overstated. From civil rights to environmental justice, young activists have proven time and again that they are the vanguards of change. As individuals of all ages, we must recognize the invaluable contributions they make and support their efforts. By doing so, we can collectively rise above the curtain of enduring inequalities, creating a society that embraces the principles of justice, equality, and opportunity for all.

TOOLS AND PLATFORMS FOR YOUTH ADVOCACY

In this ever-evolving digital age, the power of technology cannot be overlooked. It has immensely transformed the way we communicate, connect, and advocate for change. Today, young people are rising above the curtain of inequality and using various tools and platforms to amplify their voices and make a difference. This subchapter explores the incredible tools and platforms available to empower youth advocacy in the fight against enduring inequalities in society.

Social media has emerged as a powerful tool for youth advocacy. Platforms like Facebook, Twitter, and Instagram provide a space for young activists to share their stories, raise awareness, and mobilize support. Through hashtags, youth can unite around common causes, create online movements, and reach a global audience. The power of a single x (tweet) or post can ignite a fire of change and inspire others to join the fight for equality.

The Curtain That Divides US: A metaphor for society's Perpetual Inequalities.
Message for the youths

Online petition platforms, such as Change.org, have revolutionized the way young activists gather signatures and rally support for their causes. These platforms provide a simple and effective way to create and share petitions, enabling youth to demand justice, challenge discriminatory policies, and hold those in power accountable. With just a few clicks, young activists can make a significant impact and drive meaningful change.

Technology has also given rise to innovative youth-led initiatives, such as mobile apps and websites, specifically designed for advocacy. These platforms provide valuable resources, educational materials, and tools for organizing and mobilizing communities. From organizing protests to sharing educational resources, these apps and websites empower young activists to take charge of their advocacy efforts and create lasting change.

Furthermore, virtual reality (VR) and augmented reality (AR) technologies have the potential to immerse individuals in the experiences of marginalized communities, fostering empathy and understanding. Through VR and AR, young activists can create interactive stories, documentaries, and simulations that shed light on the realities faced by marginalized groups, leading to greater awareness and empathy among society.

It is essential for young activists to harness the power of these tools and platforms for effective youth advocacy. By embracing technology, they can transcend geographical boundaries, overcome systemic barriers, and build a global movement for equality.

However, it is crucial to balance virtual advocacy with real-world action, as offline efforts are equally significant in driving tangible change.

In conclusion, the tools, and platforms available for youth advocacy are vast and powerful. From social media to online petitions, mobile apps to VR technologies, young people have an unprecedented opportunity to make their voices heard and fight against enduring inequalities in society. By utilizing these tools effectively and combining them with offline activism, youth can rise above the curtain of inequality and create a more equitable and just world for all ages.

BUILDING SOLIDARITY AND COLLABORATIVE MOVEMENTS

In our journey towards dismantling the curtain that divides us and fighting the enduring inequalities in society, one powerful tool that transcends age, background, and experience is building solidarity and collaborative movements. This subchapter delves into the significance of coming together, united in purpose, to effect positive change and empower all ages to fight inequality.

Solidarity is the foundation upon which movements are built. It is the understanding that the struggles we face are interconnected, and that by standing together, we amplify our voices and increase our collective power. Solidarity bridges the gaps between generations, ethnicities, and socioeconomic statuses, reminding us that we are all in this fight against inequality together.

Collaborative movements foster an environment of inclusivity and mutual support. They provide a platform for individuals of all ages to contribute their unique perspectives, skills, and experiences. By embracing diversity within our movements, we create a powerful force capable of challenging the status quo and creating lasting change.

For the youths, understanding the importance of solidarity and collaborative movements is crucial. As the future torchbearers of change, they possess a remarkable ability to mobilize, innovate, and challenge the systems that perpetuate inequality. By nurturing their potential and providing them with platforms to express their ideas and concerns, we empower them to become leaders in their own right.

In building solidarity, we must actively listen to each other's stories and experiences. By doing so, we develop empathy and gain a deeper understanding of the various forms of inequality that exist. This shared knowledge becomes the fuel that ignites our movements, propelling us forward with a renewed sense of purpose and determination.

Collaborative movements also require effective communication and organization. By utilizing technology and social media, we can connect with individuals from all walks of life, regardless of their location or circumstances. This opens up new avenues for collaboration and allows us to build a global movement that transcends borders.

As we work towards building solidarity and collaborative movements, it is crucial to remember that change takes time. It requires patience, perseverance, and the ability to adapt to new challenges. By nurturing relationships, fostering a sense of community, and celebrating small victories along the way, we can build a movement that is resilient and sustainable.

In conclusion, building solidarity and collaborative movements is an essential step towards fighting inequality. By uniting individuals of all ages, backgrounds, and experiences, we create a powerful force capable of effecting positive change. Through active listening, inclusivity, and effective communication, we can build a movement that transcends borders, empowers the youth, and challenges the enduring inequalities that plague society. Together, we can rise above the curtain and create a more just and equitable world for all.

BUILDING RESILIENCE AND CONFIDENCE IN THE FACE OF INEQUALITY

In a world where inequality continues to persist, it is crucial for individuals of all ages to develop resilience and confidence to navigate and challenge these enduring disparities. This subchapter aims to empower readers, regardless of their age, to rise above the curtain of inequality and take action towards a more equitable society.

Firstly, it is important to acknowledge that inequality exists in various forms, including economic, racial, and gender disparities. It affects individuals across generations, limiting opportunities and perpetuating social divisions. By understanding the realities of inequality, we can begin to address its root causes and work towards creating a fairer world.

Resilience plays a vital role in combating inequality. It is the ability to bounce back from adversity and overcome obstacles. Developing resilience is a lifelong process that involves building a strong support network, fostering self-belief, and cultivating coping mechanisms. By building resilience, individuals can better withstand the challenges and setbacks that arise from living in an unequal society.

Confidence is another key ingredient in the fight against inequality. It involves believing in one's capabilities and worth and having the courage to speak up and take action. Confidence can be nurtured through education, exposure to diverse perspectives, and engaging in activities that promote self-growth. By fostering confidence, individuals can challenge societal norms, advocate for change, and inspire others to do the same.

For the youth, in particular, this subchapter offers a message of hope and empowerment. It reminds them that they have the power to shape the future and break down the barriers that perpetuate inequality. It encourages young individuals to use their voices, talents, and energy to challenge the status quo and fight for a more inclusive society.

Through personal anecdotes, real-life examples, and practical strategies, this subchapter provides guidance on how to build resilience and confidence in the face of inequality. It emphasizes the importance of self-care, self-education, allyship, and collective action. It also highlights the significance of intergenerational collaboration, as individuals of all ages can learn from each other's experiences, ideas, and perspectives.

In conclusion, building resilience and confidence is essential for individuals of all ages to effectively combat inequality. By equipping ourselves with these essential tools, we can rise above the curtain that separates us and work towards a society that values and empowers every individual, regardless of their background or circumstances. Together, we can create a more just and equitable world for all.

DEVELOPING SELF-AWARENESS AND EMPATHY

In today's world, where inequalities persist and divisions run deep, it is essential for individuals of all ages to cultivate self-awareness and empathy. This subchapter aims to guide readers through the process of developing these crucial skills, empowering them to rise above the curtain of inequality that divides us. Whether you are a young person seeking guidance or an adult looking to make a positive impact, this chapter offers insights applicable to all.

Self-awareness is the foundation upon which personal growth and societal change are built. It involves understanding our own thoughts, emotions, strengths, and weaknesses. By developing a deep understanding of ourselves, we become more aware of how our actions and words can impact others. This self-reflection allows us to challenge our biases, prejudices, and assumptions, enabling us to break free from the chains of inequality that hold us back.

Empathy, on the other hand, is the ability to understand and share the feelings of others. It is a powerful tool that fosters connection and bridges the gaps between different individuals and communities. By cultivating empathy, we can transcend our own experiences and perspectives, truly listening to and understanding the struggles faced by others. Empathy allows us to stand in solidarity with those who are marginalized, amplifying their voices, and fighting for a more equitable society.

Throughout this subchapter, readers will find practical

exercises and thought-provoking questions designed to deepen their self-awareness and empathy. From journaling prompts to role-playing scenarios, these activities will challenge readers to step outside their comfort zones and engage with the world in a more compassionate and understanding way.

Moreover, this subchapter offers insight into the enduring inequalities that persist in our society, particularly focusing on the message for the youths. It addresses the curtain that separates us, highlighting the disparities in opportunities, resources, and representation that young people face. By exploring these issues, readers will gain a comprehensive understanding of the challenges that need to be overcome, empowering them to take action and fight for a more just world.

In conclusion, developing self-awareness and empathy is essential for all ages in the fight against inequality. By understanding ourselves and extending compassion to others, we can break down barriers, challenge systemic injustices, and empower marginalized voices. This subchapter serves as a guide, providing practical tools and inspiring insights to help readers rise above the curtain that divides us and work towards a more equal and inclusive society.

The Curtain That Divides US: A metaphor for society's Perpetual Inequalities. Message for the youths

OVERCOMING STEREOTYPES AND SELF-LIMITING BELIEFS

In a world plagued by inequality, it is essential for all ages to rise above the barriers that separate us and break free from the shackles of stereotypes and self-limiting beliefs. This subchapter aims to empower individuals of all ages, particularly the youth, to challenge societal norms, question ingrained prejudices, and unleash their true potential.

Stereotypes have long been used to categorize and pigeonhole individuals, often leading to discrimination and exclusion. Whether based on gender, race, age, or any other characteristic, these preconceived notions limit our understanding and hinder our ability to form meaningful connections. It is crucial to recognize that everyone is unique, with their own talents, dreams, and aspirations. By breaking free from stereotypes, we can embrace diversity and create a more inclusive society.

Self-limiting beliefs are the internal barriers that hold us back from achieving our goals and reaching our full potential. These beliefs are often deeply ingrained, acquired through negative experiences or societal conditioning. They whisper in our minds, telling us that we are not good enough, smart enough, or deserving of success. However, it is important to remember that these beliefs are not grounded in reality. By challenging and overcoming these self-imposed limitations, we can unlock our true capabilities and accomplish great things.

To overcome stereotypes and self-limiting beliefs, it is crucial to foster a mindset of openness, empathy, and self-reflection. By actively seeking to understand others and their experiences, we can challenge our own biases and assumptions. Engaging in dialogue and cultivating a sense of curiosity will help us break down the barriers that divide us and foster a more inclusive and understanding society.

Empowering the youth is vital in the fight against inequality. By providing them with the tools to challenge stereotypes and self-limiting beliefs, we can create a generation that is unafraid to dream big and reshape the world. Education, mentorship, and exposure to diverse perspectives are essential in instilling confidence and resilience in our young minds.

In conclusion, overcoming stereotypes and self-limiting beliefs is a powerful act that can transform both individuals and society as a whole. By embracing diversity, challenging preconceived notions, and empowering the youth, we can rise above the curtain of inequality, creating a world where everyone is valued and given equal opportunities to thrive. Let us break free from the chains that hold us back and rewrite the narrative of our lives, paving the way for a brighter and more inclusive future.

NURTURING LEADERSHIP AND CIVIC ENGAGEMENTS SKILLS

In a world where enduring inequalities continue to divide us, it is crucial to nurture leadership and civic engagement skills among people of all ages. This subchapter aims to empower individuals and provide them with the tools necessary to fight against these inequalities. By understanding the curtain that divides us and the unique message it holds for the youth, we can create a more inclusive and equitable society.

Leadership is not limited to a particular age group or position of authority; it is a mindset and a set of skills that can be cultivated by anyone. Through this subchapter, we will explore various strategies and techniques to foster leadership qualities. By encouraging individuals to take initiative, think critically, and inspire others, we can empower them to become agents of change in their communities. Leadership development programs, mentorship opportunities, and experiential learning activities will be discussed, emphasizing the importance of practical experience in shaping effective leaders.

Civic engagement is another vital component in the fight against inequality. It encourages individuals to actively participate in their communities, understand social issues, and work towards their resolution. This subchapter will provide concrete examples of how people of all ages can engage in civic activities, whether through volunteering, advocacy, or community organizing. By highlighting successful grassroots movements and initiatives, we aim to inspire readers to take action and make a difference.

The message for the youth is particularly important in addressing enduring inequalities. Young people possess the passion, energy, and fresh perspective needed to challenge the status quo. This subchapter will emphasize the importance of youth involvement in leadership and civic engagement, highlighting inspiring stories of young leaders who have made a significant impact on their communities. It will also provide guidance on how young people can overcome obstacles and navigate societal barriers to create positive change.

This subchapter aims to empower individuals of all ages to rise above the curtain of enduring inequalities and fight for a more equitable society. By nurturing leadership qualities and encouraging civic engagement, we can create a generation of change-makers who are committed to breaking down barriers and promoting inclusivity. Through education, inspiration, and practical guidance, we can empower individuals to make a lasting impact and create a more just world for all.

CHAPTER 3: BREAKING DOWN THE CURTAIN: STRATEGIES FOR ALL AGES

PROMOTING ECONOMIC EQUALITY AND FINANCIAL LITERACY

In an era marked by persistent inequalities, it is imperative that we equip ourselves with the knowledge and tools necessary to fight against these disparities. Economic equality and financial literacy are two key areas where we can empower ourselves and others, regardless of our age, to rise above the curtain that divides us.

Financial literacy is the foundation upon which economic equality can be built. It encompasses the knowledge and skills needed to make informed decisions about money, budgeting, saving, and investing. By promoting financial literacy among all ages, we can ensure that individuals have the necessary tools to navigate the complex world of finance and make excellent financial decisions.

For the younger generation, it is crucial to instill financial literacy early on. Teaching children about money management, saving, and budgeting empowers them to develop responsible financial habits from an early age. By equipping our youth with these essential skills, we can help break the cycle of poverty and inequality that often persists across generations.

However, financial literacy is not limited to the young. Individuals of all ages can benefit from ongoing education and support in this area. Many adults find themselves struggling with debt, living paycheck to paycheck, or lacking the knowledge to make sound financial decisions. By providing accessible resources and education on financial literacy, we can empower adults to take control of their financial futures and work towards economic equality.

Promoting economic equality goes beyond financial literacy alone. It requires addressing the systemic barriers and inequalities that perpetuate economic disparities.

Governments, organizations, and individuals must collaborate to create an inclusive society that provides equal opportunities for all. This includes advocating for fair wages, affordable housing, access to quality education, and healthcare.

By promoting economic equality and financial literacy, we can break down the curtain that separates us and build a more just and equitable society. It is a message that resonates with all ages, as we all have a stake in creating a fairer world. Let us empower ourselves and others to rise above the inequalities that persist, and together, we can build a brighter future for everyone.

REDUCING THE WEALTH GAP AND INCOME INEQUALITY

In today's society, the wealth gap and income inequality continue to be pressing issues that affect people of all ages. The curtain that separates us, the enduring inequalities in society, have a profound impact on our lives, and it is crucial that we address these disparities for the betterment of our communities. This subchapter aims to shed light on the causes of wealth gaps and income inequality and provide practical solutions for all ages to fight against these injustices.

The wealth gap refers to the unequal distribution of assets and resources among individuals or groups. It is often a result of systemic factors such as discrimination, lack of access to quality education and healthcare, and limited economic opportunities.

Similarly, income inequality arises from disparities in wages and salaries, reinforcing the wealth gap and perpetuating social and economic inequalities.

To tackle these issues, it is essential for all ages to understand the root causes and actively work towards reducing the wealth gap and income inequality. Education plays a pivotal role in empowering individuals to fight against these injustices. By raising awareness about the impact of these disparities and providing tools and resources, we can equip people of all ages with the knowledge to challenge systemic inequalities.

Furthermore, advocating for policy changes is crucial in reducing the wealth gap and income inequality. It is imperative for individuals of all ages to engage in grassroots movements, lobby for fair taxation, and support policies that promote economic justice. By actively participating in civic and political processes, we can create an environment that fosters equal opportunities for everyone.

Additionally, fostering economic empowerment is essential in reducing the wealth gap. Encouraging entrepreneurship, providing access to financial education, and supporting small businesses are effective ways to promote economic mobility and bridge the income gap. By creating a level playing field, we can empower individuals and communities to thrive and overcome financial disparities.

In conclusion, reducing the wealth gap and income inequality requires collective action from people of all ages. By understanding the root causes, advocating for policy changes, and fostering economic empowerment, we can work towards a fairer and more inclusive society. It is vital for us to rise above the curtain of enduring inequalities and empower future generations to fight against these systemic injustices. Together, we can create a world where everyone has equal opportunities to succeed and thrive, regardless of their age or background.

STRENGTHENING SOCIAL SAFETY NETS

In a society plagued by enduring inequalities, it is crucial to address the disparities that separate us. One effective way to combat these inequalities is by strengthening social safety nets. This subchapter delves into the importance of bolstering these safety nets and highlights the message it holds for individuals of all ages, especially the youth.

Social safety nets are programs and policies designed to provide support, assistance, and protection to individuals and families facing economic hardships. These safety nets aim to ensure that no one falls through the cracks, regardless of their age, race, gender, or socioeconomic background. By strengthening these safety nets, we can create a more equitable society where everyone has access to necessities and opportunities.

For the youth, the message behind strengthening social safety nets is empowering. It sends a clear signal that their well-being and future matter. By investing in social programs such as affordable education, healthcare, and job training, we provide young people with the tools they need to overcome obstacles and achieve their full potential. It also sends a message of hope, assuring them that their dreams are not limited by their circumstances.

Moreover, strengthening social safety nets benefits individuals of all ages. As we age, we become more vulnerable to economic uncertainties, health issues, and social isolation. Robust safety nets can provide a sense of security and peace of mind for older adults, ensuring they are not left behind or forgotten.

This subchapter explores various strategies to strengthen social safety nets, including advocating for comprehensive healthcare coverage, affordable housing initiatives, income support programs, and access to quality education. It also emphasizes the importance of community engagement and partnerships to address these enduring inequalities collectively.

Ultimately, strengthening social safety nets requires a collective effort from individuals, communities, and policymakers. It demands a commitment to creating an inclusive society that values the well-being of all its members. By reading this subchapter, individuals of all ages can gain a deeper understanding of the importance of social safety nets and the role they play in fighting inequality. It empowers readers to become advocates for change and encourages them to take action in their own lives and communities.

The subsection, "Strengthening Social Safety Nets" addresses the enduring inequalities in society and delivers a powerful message to individuals of all ages. It emphasizes the importance of investing in social programs, empowering the youth, and creating a more equitable society. By understanding the significance of social safety nets and taking collective action, we can rise above the curtain of inequality, empower all ages, and build a better future for everyone.

EMPOWERING INDIVIDUALS THROUGH FINANCIAL EDUCATION

In today's rapidly changing world, financial literacy has

become an essential skill for individuals of all ages. The ability to understand and manage finances not only empowers individuals to make informed decisions but also serves as a catalyst for breaking down the enduring inequalities in society. In this subchapter, we will explore the significance of financial education and its potential to empower individuals across all age groups.

Financial education is more than just understanding numbers and balancing budgets; it is about equipping individuals with the knowledge and skills necessary to navigate the complexities of the financial world. Whether you are a young student learning the basics of money management or an adult striving for financial independence, understanding how to budget, save, invest, and protect your assets is crucial. By providing individuals with the tools and knowledge to make sound financial decisions, we can break free from the constraints of inequality and build a more inclusive society.

For the youths, the curtain that separates us from achieving equality often manifests in limited access to financial resources, lack of guidance, and misinformation about financial matters. This subchapter aims to bridge this gap by providing valuable insights and practical advice to empower young individuals to overcome financial obstacles and make informed choices. It will address critical topics such as creating a budget, managing debt, saving for the future, and understanding the importance of credit.

Financial education is not limited to any specific age group; it is a lifelong journey of learning and adapting. Therefore, this subchapter will also provide valuable insights for adults, highlighting the importance of continuous learning and adaptation to changing economic landscapes. It will delve into topics such as retirement planning, investment strategies, and the significance of financial resilience during uncertain times.

By empowering individuals through financial education, we can begin to dismantle the curtain of inequality that separates us. Regardless of age, financial literacy provides the tools to overcome financial challenges, make informed decisions, and build a better future. This subchapter serves as a guiding light, offering practical advice, valuable insights, and inspiring stories to empower all ages to fight against inequality and take control of their financial well-being. Together, we can rise above the curtain and create a more inclusive and prosperous society for all.

The Curtain That Divides US: A metaphor for society's Perpetual Inequalities. Message for the youths

ADDRESSING SOCIAL INEQUALITY: CHALLENGING DISCRIMINATION

In a world that claims to value equality and justice for all, social inequality and discrimination continue to persist in various forms. This subchapter aims to shed light on these enduring inequalities that act as a curtain, separating individuals and communities, and provide a message of empowerment for the youths who hold the power to challenge and dismantle these discriminatory systems.

Social inequality is a multifaceted issue that encompasses economic, racial, gender, and social disparities. It hampers the progress of individuals and communities, limiting their opportunities and perpetuating a cycle of disadvantage. It is crucial for all ages to understand the deep-rooted nature of these inequalities and actively work towards their eradication.

One aspect of social inequality is racial discrimination, which continues to marginalize certain groups based on their skin color or ethnic background. It is essential to recognize the harm caused by racial prejudice and challenge the stereotypes and biases that perpetuate discrimination. By fostering inclusivity and embracing diversity, we can break down the barriers that hinder social progress.

The Curtain That Divides US: A metaphor for society's Perpetual Inequalities.
Message for the youths

Gender inequality is another significant form of discrimination that affects people of all ages. Women and girls often face unequal access to education, employment opportunities, and healthcare. Empowering women and advocating for gender equality is not only a matter of justice but also a catalyst for social and economic development. It is crucial to educate all ages about the importance of gender equality and challenge the societal norms and expectations that restrict individuals based on their gender.

Economic inequality, characterized by the unequal distribution of wealth and resources, is yet another form of social disparity. It widens the gap between the rich and the poor, limiting opportunities for upward mobility and perpetuating social exclusion. By advocating for fair taxation, access to quality education, and a living wage for all, we can strive towards a more equitable society.

To address social inequality effectively, it is imperative to empower the youths, who hold the potential to challenge and dismantle discriminatory systems. Education plays a crucial role in shaping their understanding of social issues and equipping them with the tools to effect change. By providing platforms for dialogue, encouraging critical thinking, and promoting activism, we can inspire the younger generation to rise above the curtain of inequality and work towards a more just and inclusive society.

In conclusion, addressing social inequality and challenging discrimination is a collective responsibility that requires the active participation of all ages. By understanding the enduring inequalities that separate us and empowering the youths to fight against them, we can break down the barriers and create an equitable and inclusive world for all. It is time to rise above the curtain of inequality and work towards a future where justice and equality prevails.

PROMOTING INCLUSIVE POLICIES AND LEGISLATION

In a world where inequalities persist, it is essential to address the curtain that divides us and empower individuals of all ages to fight against it. The subchapter "Promoting Inclusive Policies and Legislation" aims to shed light on the importance of creating a fair and just society for everyone, while specifically targeting the youth who will shape the future. By understanding and actively participating in the process of promoting inclusive policies and legislation, we can collectively work towards dismantling the barriers that hinder progress.

Inclusive policies and legislation serve as powerful tools to combat inequality. They are designed to ensure that no individual or group is left behind, irrespective of age, gender, race, or socioeconomic background. By implementing these policies, governments and organizations can actively work towards leveling the playing field and creating equal opportunities for all. This subchapter delves into the significance of inclusive policies and legislation and their impact on society.

Through this subchapter, readers of all ages will gain a deeper understanding of the systematic inequalities that exist in our society. By exploring various case studies and real-life examples, we highlight the pressing need for change. We discuss the detrimental effects of inequality on individuals and communities, emphasizing the urgency to address these issues head-on.

The subchapter also provides insights into how individuals, regardless of age, can actively participate in promoting inclusive policies and legislation. We discuss the importance of civic engagement, encouraging readers to use their voices to advocate for change. By utilizing various platforms such as social media, community organizations, and grassroots movements, individuals can join the fight against inequality and make a lasting impact.

"Promoting Inclusive Policies and Legislation" is a guide

on how to navigate the complexities of policymaking. We provide readers with a step-by- step approach to understanding the legislative process, effectively lobbying for change, and collaborating with policymakers. By empowering individuals with this knowledge, we equip them with the tools necessary to make a difference in their communities.

Overall, this subchapter serves as a rallying call to individuals of all ages to rise above the curtain of inequality. By promoting inclusive policies and legislation, we can collectively work towards building a fair and just society for all. It is our hope that this chapter inspires readers to take action, igniting a movement that will create lasting change for generations to come.

FOSTERING DIVERSITY AND INCLUSION IN COMMUNITIES

In today's increasingly interconnected world, it is more important than ever to foster diversity and inclusion in our communities. The curtain that divides us, the enduring inequalities in society, can only be dismantled by empowering all ages to fight against this injustice. In this subchapter, we will explore the significance of diversity and inclusion, and how they can contribute to creating a more equitable and harmonious society.

Diversity refers to human differences, including but not limited to race, ethnicity, gender, age, sexual orientation, and abilities. Inclusion, on the other hand, is the practice of ensuring that all individuals feel a sense of belonging in a society and feel valued and respected in the community. By embracing diversity and fostering inclusion, we can celebrate the unique qualities and perspectives that each individual brings to the table.

One of the key benefits of diversity and inclusion is the richness of ideas and experiences they bring. When people from different backgrounds come together, their diverse perspectives can lead to creative problem-solving and innovation. By promoting diversity and inclusion, we can tap into the collective wisdom of our communities and find more effective solutions to the enduring inequalities that plague our society.

Furthermore, fostering diversity and inclusion can help break down the barriers that divide us. By recognizing and appreciating the value of everyone, regardless of their differences, we can create a sense of belonging and unity. This not only strengthens our communities but also promotes social cohesion and harmony.

For the youths, understanding the importance of diversity

and inclusion is crucial. They are the future leaders and change-makers who will shape the world. By instilling in them the values of equality and inclusivity, we can empower them to challenge the enduring inequalities and work towards a fairer society. It is essential to provide them with the knowledge, skills, and opportunities to foster diversity and inclusion in their communities actively.

In conclusion, fostering diversity and inclusion in communities is a fundamental step towards fighting the enduring inequalities in society. By celebrating our differences and creating a sense of belonging for all individuals, we can break down the curtain that separates us. Empowering all ages, particularly the youths, to embrace diversity and promote inclusion is vital for creating a more equitable and just world. Together, we can rise above the curtain and build a society where everyone has an equal opportunity to thrive.

ENCOURAGING EMPATHY AND UNDERSTANDING

In a world plagued by enduring inequalities, fostering empathy and understanding is crucial in our collective fight against injustice. This subchapter aims to empower readers of all ages, particularly the youth, to rise above the metaphorical curtain that separates us and embrace a more compassionate and inclusive society.

Empathy is the ability to understand and share the feelings of others. It is a powerful tool that allows us to connect with people from diverse backgrounds, enabling us to bridge divides and dismantle the barriers that perpetuate inequality. By encouraging empathy, we can cultivate a society that values the unique experiences and perspectives of each individual.

One way to foster empathy is through education and exposure to different cultures, experiences, and perspectives. Through literature, art, and various media platforms, we can introduce readers of all ages to stories that challenge their preconceived notions and widen their understanding of the world. By encouraging open-mindedness and curiosity, we empower individuals to question their own biases and embrace a more inclusive mindset.

Furthermore, promoting empathy requires active listening and meaningful conversations. By creating safe spaces for dialogue, we encourage individuals to share their experiences, fears, and dreams. By truly listening to others, we validate their experiences and emotions, fostering a sense of understanding and connection.

These conversations can inspire action, as we collectively work towards dismantling the barriers that separate us.

Empathy is also closely tied to education and awareness. By teaching young minds about the historical and contemporary injustices that have shaped our society, we equip them with the knowledge needed to challenge and change the status quo. Through education, we can cultivate a generation that actively seeks to create a more equitable world, championing the rights of marginalized communities.

In conclusion, encouraging empathy and understanding is paramount in our fight against enduring inequalities. By promoting empathy through education, exposure, and meaningful conversations, we can break down the metaphorical curtain that separates us. This subchapter empowers readers of all ages, particularly the youth, to rise above societal divisions and work towards a society that embraces diversity, inclusivity, and equal opportunity for all. Together, we can create a more compassionate and just world for future generations to come.

The Curtain That Divides US: A metaphor for society's Perpetual Inequalities.
Message for the youths

CREATING AN EQUITABLE SOCIETY: POLICY AND SYSTEMIC CHANGES

In a world plagued by deep-rooted social inequalities, it is imperative that we address the curtain that separates us and work towards creating an equitable society. This subchapter delves into the importance of policy and systemic changes in combating these enduring inequalities, with a particular focus on empowering the youths.

To truly overcome the barriers that divide us, we must recognize the role of policies in shaping our society. Policies have the power to either perpetuate or dismantle inequality. By advocating for policy changes that prioritize social justice, we can make significant strides towards creating a more equitable society. This includes policies that address income disparities, access to quality education, healthcare, and affordable housing. It is crucial to involve individuals of all ages in the policy-making process, as their unique perspectives and experiences can shed light on the diverse needs of our society.

Systemic changes are equally vital in dismantling the curtain that separates us. Our systems, whether economic, political, or social, often perpetuate inequality without us even realizing it. By critically examining and challenging these systems, we can begin to dismantle the barriers that limit equal opportunities for all. This requires a collaboration among individuals, communities, and institutions. It involves reevaluating our biases, promoting inclusivity, and fostering empathy towards marginalized groups.

For the youths, understanding and actively engaging in the fight against inequality is crucial. They are the future leaders and change-makers and empowering them with knowledge and tools to address social injustices is paramount. By educating young people about the enduring inequalities in society, we can ignite a passion for creating change. We must nurture their empathy and encourage their active participation in initiatives that challenge the status quo.

Furthermore, it is essential to emphasize the interconnectedness of various forms of inequality. Addressing one aspect, such as gender inequality, without considering its intersectionality with race, socioeconomic status, or ability, is insufficient and will not resolve the problem. By adopting an intersectional approach, we can ensure that our efforts to create an equitable society are comprehensive and inclusive.

In conclusion, creating an equitable society requires both policy changes and systemic shifts. It necessitates the active involvement of individuals of all ages, with a particular focus on empowering the youths. By advocating for policies that prioritize social justice and challenging the systems that perpetuate inequality, we can work towards tearing down the curtain that separates us. Let us unite in our fight against enduring inequalities, fostering empathy, and empowering all ages to rise above the curtain.

ADVOCATING FOR FAIRNESS IN EDUCATION SYSTEMS

Education is the cornerstone of any society, shaping the minds and futures of individuals. However, it is disheartening to acknowledge that our education systems often perpetuate inequalities, leaving countless individuals behind. In this subchapter, we delve into the importance of advocating for fairness in education systems, addressing the enduring inequalities that exist within society, and delivering a powerful message to the youth.

Education is meant to be the great equalizer, providing everyone with an opportunity to succeed regardless of their background. Unfortunately, the curtain of inequality has prevented many from accessing quality education. It is our duty, as a society, to tear down this curtain and create a fair and equitable education system for all.

The Curtain That Divides US: A metaphor for society's Perpetual Inequalities.
Message for the youths

One of the key aspects of advocating for fairness in education systems is addressing the disparities that exist within the system itself. We must challenge the discrepancies in resource allocation, teacher quality, and curriculum development. By advocating for increased funding for schools in underserved communities, ensuring highly qualified teachers in all classrooms, and promoting inclusive and diverse curricula, we can begin to level the playing field.

Furthermore, it is crucial to recognize the societal inequalities that influence educational outcomes. Income disparity, racial discrimination, and gender biases all play a significant role in determining access to quality education. By advocating for policies that combat these inequalities head-on, we can create an environment where everyone has an equal opportunity to thrive academically.

In delivering this message to the youth, we aim to inspire and empower them to fight against inequality. We must encourage them to question the status quo, challenge prejudices, and advocate for change within their educational institutions. By fostering a sense of agency and activism, we can ensure that the next generation becomes the catalyst for a fairer and more just education system.

It is important for all ages to recognize that advocating for fairness in education systems is not only a moral imperative but also a necessary step towards building a more equitable society. By providing equal access to education, we unlock the potential of individuals who may otherwise be left behind, contributing to the overall progress and development of our communities.

In conclusion, advocating for fairness in education systems is a crucial step in dismantling the enduring inequalities that plague our society. By addressing the disparities within the education system itself and challenging the societal factors that influence educational outcomes, we can create a more just and inclusive society.

Empowering all ages, especially the youth, to fight against inequality in education is the key to overcoming the curtain that separates us and building a brighter future for all.

RETHINKING CRIMINAL JUSTICE AND PRISON REFORM

In the contemporary world, it is crucial for all ages to engage in a critical examination of the criminal justice system and ponder the dire need for prison reform. This subchapter delves into the multifaceted issues surrounding criminal justice and offers a thought-provoking perspective on how we can rise above the curtain of inequality and work towards a fairer society.

The current criminal justice system often perpetuates enduring inequalities within society. It disproportionately affects marginalized communities, such as people of color and those from low-income backgrounds, who find themselves trapped in a cycle of incarceration. We must acknowledge this systemic injustice and strive for change.

To begin with, rehabilitation should be at the forefront of our prison system. Rather than focusing solely on punishment, we need to prioritize the reformation and reintegration of offenders into society. By offering educational programs, vocational training, mental health support, and substance abuse treatment, we can empower individuals to break free from the cycle of crime and contribute positively to their communities.

Furthermore, we must address the issue of mass incarceration. The United States, for instance, has the highest incarceration rate in the world, with overcrowded prisons and disproportionately lengthy sentences. Implementing alternative sentencing options, such as community service, restorative justice, and probation, can help reduce the strain on prisons and provide more effective outcomes for both individuals and society.

Additionally, youth involvement in the criminal justice system demands special attention. We need to invest in early intervention programs that focus on prevention rather than punishment. By providing at-risk young people with mentorship, support, and access to educational opportunities, we can steer them away from a life of crime and give them a chance to build a brighter future.

Ultimately, rethinking criminal justice and prison reform requires a collective effort involving all ages. By engaging in open discussions, advocating for policy changes, and supporting organizations dedicated to criminal justice reform, we can dismantle the curtain of inequality that separates us. Together, we have the power to create a society that emphasizes fairness, rehabilitation, and a genuine commitment to reducing crime.

In conclusion, this subchapter challenges all ages to rethink criminal justice and prison reform. By acknowledging the enduring inequalities within our society and advocating for change, we can actively work towards a more just and equitable future. Let us rise above the curtain of inequality and empower both ourselves and the next generation to fight for a criminal justice system that truly serves the interests of all.

PROMOTING EQUAL OPPORTUNITIES IN EMPLOYMENT

In today's society, the pursuit of equality has become an urgent and essential task. The subchapter "Promoting Equal Opportunities in Employment" delves into the significance of creating a level playing field for all individuals, regardless of their age, background, or circumstances. It aims to inspire readers of all ages, particularly those interested in understanding and addressing the enduring inequalities that exist within our society.

Employment is a fundamental aspect of our lives, shaping our sense of self-worth, financial stability, and overall well-being. Unfortunately, many individuals still face barriers in accessing equal opportunities in the workforce. Discrimination based on age, gender, race, or socioeconomic class limits their chances of securing meaningful employment and reaching their full potential.

This subchapter explores various strategies and initiatives that can be implemented to promote equal opportunities in employment. It emphasizes the importance of education and awareness in challenging societal prejudices and stereotypes. By understanding the value of diversity and inclusivity, we can foster workplaces that empower individuals from all walks of life.

The chapter highlights the significance of legislation and policies that protect against discrimination and promote equal treatment in the workplace. It calls upon policymakers, business leaders, and individuals alike to advocate for fair hiring practices, equal pay, and opportunities for career advancement. Furthermore, it sheds light on the role of mentorship programs, internships, and vocational training in bridging the gap between individuals and employment opportunities.

Addressing the youth directly, this subchapter emphasizes the importance of cultivating a generation that is passionate about fighting inequality. It encourages young people to be proactive in challenging stereotypes, creating inclusive spaces, and advocating for equal opportunities in employment. By empowering the youth, we can ensure a future where equality is not just an aspiration, but a reality.

"Promoting Equal Opportunities in Employment" is a call to action, inspiring readers of all ages to recognize the enduring inequalities within our society and take steps towards dismantling them. It provides practical strategies, real-life examples, and thought- provoking insights to motivate individuals to make a difference in their own lives and communities.

By rising above the curtain of inequality, we can create a world where everyone, regardless of their age, gender, or background, has an equal chance to succeed and thrive. Together, let us empower all ages to fight inequality and build a brighter future for generations to come.

CHAPTER 4: RISING ABOVE THE CURTAIN: INSPIRING STORIES OF CHANGE

YOUTH-LED INITIATIVES: MAKING A DIFFERENCE

In today's world, the curtain that separates us, the enduring inequalities in society, remains a pressing issue that affects people of all ages. While governments, organizations, and individuals strive to address these inequalities, it is the youth-led initiatives that are making a significant difference. These young individuals are rising above the curtain, empowering themselves and others to fight against inequality.

The power of youth-led initiatives lies in the passion, determination, and fresh perspectives that young people bring to the table. They refuse to accept the status quo and are driven to create a more inclusive and fair society. These initiatives cover a wide range of issues, from gender equality and climate change to education and poverty alleviation.

One of the key messages for the youth is that they have

the power to make a difference, regardless of their age or background. They are not just the leaders of tomorrow; they are the leaders of today. By taking action and raising their voices, they can challenge the inequalities that persist in our society.

Youth-led initiatives often start small, with a group of like-minded individuals coming together to address a particular issue. They use their creativity and innovation to develop solutions that are both effective and sustainable. Through grassroots campaigns, social media advocacy, and community engagement, they are able to mobilize support and raise awareness about the inequalities that are often overlooked.

One inspiring example of a youth-led initiative is the movement for climate justice. Young activists such as Greta Thunberg have captured the world's attention, demanding urgent action to combat climate change. Their voices have resonated with people of all ages, inspiring millions to join the fight for a sustainable future. Through protests, strikes, and lobbying efforts, these young activists have forced governments and corporations to take notice and make concrete changes.

Another remarkable youth-led initiative is the fight for education equality. Many young individuals have recognized the importance of education in breaking the cycle of poverty and inequality. They have established programs to provide educational opportunities to marginalized communities, ensuring that every child has access to quality education, regardless of their socioeconomic background.

The message for the youth is clear: they have the power to make a difference. By leading initiatives and mobilizing communities, they can challenge the enduring inequalities in society. It is through their passion, determination, and unwavering belief in a better future that real change can be achieved.

In conclusion, youth-led initiatives are playing a crucial role in breaking down the curtain that separates us and fighting against enduring inequalities. Their creativity, innovation, and determination are making a significant difference in addressing a wide range of issues. The message for the youth is that they have the power to create change, and it is through their actions that a more inclusive and fair society can be built. Let us all support and empower the youth in their endeavors, for together, we can rise above the curtain and create a world where equality reigns.

SUCCESS STORIES OF YOUTH-LED MOVEMENTS

One such success story is the youth-led movement for climate justice. Concerned about the devastating effects of climate change on the planet and future generations, young activists around the world have taken to the streets, demanding urgent action from governments and corporations. Their relentless advocacy has brought the climate crisis to the forefront of global discussions, leading to significant policy changes and commitments to reduce carbon emissions. Through their determination and unwavering voice, these young activists have shown that age is not a barrier to making a difference.

Another inspiring success story is the youth-led movements for racial equality. In the face of systemic racism and discrimination, young activists have mobilized their communities and raised awareness about the injustices faced by marginalized groups. Through peaceful protests, social media campaigns, and community organizing, they have forced conversations about racial inequality and prompted governments to take concrete steps towards dismantling discriminatory practices. These movements have highlighted the power of youth in challenging the status quo and demanding a more inclusive society.

The success stories of youth-led movements also extend to gender equality. Young activists have been at the forefront of advocating for women's rights and gender justice. From fighting against gender-based violence to promoting equal opportunities for women in education and employment, these movements have sparked a global conversation about gender equality. Through their efforts, they have not only empowered individuals but also encouraged societies to recognize the importance of gender equality in creating a more just and equitable world.

These success stories serve as a message for youths and people of all ages. They demonstrate that change is possible, and that it often starts with the actions of passionate individuals. They remind us that we all have a role to play in fighting inequality and breaking down the barriers that separate us. Whether through activism, education, or simply challenging our own biases, we can contribute to creating a more inclusive and equal society.

In conclusion, the success stories of youth-led movements are a testament to the power of collective action and the ability of young individuals to drive meaningful change. They inspire people of all ages to rise above the curtain of enduring inequalities and work towards a more just and equitable world. Let these stories be a call to action for all, urging us to join hands and empower each other in the fight against inequality.

LESSONS LEARNED AND STRATEGIES FOR SUCCESS

In the subchapter from the book titled "The Curtain That Divides US: A metaphor for society's Perpetual Inequalities. Message for the youths" we aim to provide valuable insights and practical strategies to address the enduring inequalities in society, with a special message for the youths.

Throughout history, societies have grappled with various forms of inequality, creating a curtain that divides us. This curtain prevents individuals from reaching their full potential and living in a just and inclusive world. However, it is crucial to recognize that change is possible, and by working together, we can overcome these inequalities.

One of the most important lessons we have learned is the power of education. Education is not just about acquiring knowledge; it empowers us to challenge the status quo and envision a fairer society. By investing in education, we can equip individuals of all ages with the tools they need to fight inequality and create positive change.

Another key lesson is the importance of empathy and understanding. By stepping into the shoes of others, we can develop a deep sense of compassion and recognize the struggles faced by those who are marginalized. This empathy enables us to become advocates for equality and work towards dismantling the barriers that separate us.

To succeed in this fight against inequality, we must adopt a multi-pronged approach. This includes promoting diversity and inclusion in all aspects of society, ensuring equal opportunities for all, and actively working to eliminate discrimination. By embracing diversity, we can tap into a wealth of perspectives and experiences, ultimately fostering a more inclusive and equitable society.

Furthermore, it is essential to empower the youth as agents of change. The younger generation holds immense potential to challenge and disrupt the existing inequalities. We must provide them with platforms to voice their concerns, engage in meaningful dialogue, and actively participate in decision-making processes. By supporting and encouraging the youth, we can foster a sense of ownership and drive lasting change.

In conclusion, the subchapter "Lessons Learned and

Strategies for Success" emphasizes the need to address the enduring inequalities in society. By investing in education, promoting empathy, embracing diversity, and empowering the youth, we can break down the curtain that separates us. Let us work together across all ages and niches to fight inequality and create a more just and inclusive world for all.

SUSTAINING AND SCALING UP YOUTH INITIATIVES

In a world where inequalities persist and the curtain that separates us seems insurmountable, the power of youth initiatives to fight against these enduring inequalities cannot be underestimated. The energy, passion, and creativity of young people have the potential to create lasting change and break down barriers that have divided societies for generations. However, for these initiatives to be truly impactful, they need to be sustained and scaled up.

Sustainability is crucial to ensure that youth initiatives continue to thrive and make a difference in the long run. Often, these initiatives start with great enthusiasm and momentum but struggle to maintain their momentum over time. To sustain youth initiatives, it is important to establish strong foundations that include clear goals, effective leadership, and adequate resources. Additionally, fostering collaboration and partnerships with other organizations, both within and outside the youth sector, can provide the necessary support and expertise to sustain these initiatives. By building a strong network of like-minded individuals and organizations, youth initiatives can draw upon a range of resources and expertise, ensuring their longevity and impact.

Scaling up is equally important to maximize the reach and influence of youth initiatives. While local projects and initiatives can have a significant impact on a small scale, scaling up ensures that their effects are magnified and reach a wider audience. This can be achieved by replicating successful projects in different communities, regions, or even countries. Sharing best practices and lessons learned through networking, conferences, and workshops can help inspire and empower young people to adapt and implement similar initiatives in their own contexts. Additionally, leveraging technology and social media platforms can exponentially increase the visibility and influence of youth initiatives, allowing them to transcend geographical boundaries and inspire change on a global scale.

To truly empower all ages in the fight against inequality, it is essential to send a strong message to the youths. The curtain that separates us, the enduring inequalities in society, can only be dismantled by the collective efforts of all individuals, regardless of age. Encouraging and supporting youth initiatives not only amplifies their voices but also demonstrates a belief in their ability to shape a more equitable future. By investing in the education, mentorship, and resources necessary for young people to develop and sustain their initiatives, we can create an environment conducive to their growth and success.

In conclusion, sustaining and scaling up youth initiatives is vital in the ongoing battle against inequality. By establishing strong foundations, fostering collaboration, and leveraging technology, these initiatives can have a lasting impact and inspire change on a global scale. Empowering all ages to fight inequality requires us to acknowledge the potential of young people and provide them with the necessary support and resources. Together, we can tear down the curtain that separates us and create a more equitable society for all.

The Curtain That Divides US: A metaphor for society's Perpetual Inequalities.
Message for the youths

INTERGENERATIONAL COLLABORATION: BRIDGING THE GAP

In a world that often seems divided by age, it is crucial to recognize the power of intergenerational collaboration as a means to bridge the gap and fight against inequality. This subchapter explores the importance of uniting people of all ages to address the enduring inequalities in society and sends a powerful message to the youths of today.

Society is often characterized by a metaphorical curtain that divides different age groups, leading to misunderstandings, stereotypes, and missed opportunities for growth and progress. However, when people of all ages come together, they can break down this curtain and build a stronger, more inclusive community.

Intergenerational collaboration is a two-way street, offering benefits for both younger and older individuals. Young people bring energy, enthusiasm, and fresh perspectives, while older generations offer wisdom, experience, and guidance. By combining these strengths, we can create a powerful force for change.

One of the key messages for the youths is that they have the power to challenge and overcome the perpetual inequalities in our society. Empowering them with knowledge, skills, and opportunities to engage with different generations can inspire them to take action and become agents of change. Through intergenerational collaboration, youths can learn from the experiences of their elders and gain a deeper understanding of the issues they face, thus equipping themselves with the tools to fight inequality more effectively.

Furthermore, intergenerational collaboration can help break down stereotypes and challenge ageist attitudes. By working side by side, older and younger individuals can learn from each other's unique perspectives, dispelling misconceptions and fostering empathy and respect.

This subchapter will provide practical examples of successful intergenerational collaborations and highlight the positive impact they have had on various communities. It will also offer strategies and tools for individuals and organizations to facilitate and promote intergenerational collaboration in their own lives and work.

In conclusion, intergenerational collaboration is a powerful tool for bridging the gap between age groups and fighting against enduring inequalities. By uniting people of all ages, we can break down barriers, challenge stereotypes, and empower the youths to become catalysts for change. Together, we can rise above the curtain and create a more equitable and inclusive society for all.

THE POWER OF INTERGENERATIONAL MENTORSHIP

In a world that often feels divided by age, where the young and the old are seen as separate entities, there lies an untapped source of immense power - intergenerational mentorship. It is a concept that holds the potential to bridge the gap between generations, empower individuals of all ages, and create a society that thrives on the strength of its collective wisdom.

Intergenerational mentorship is not limited to the transfer of knowledge from older to younger individuals. It is a reciprocal relationship that benefits both parties involved, allowing for the exchange of ideas, experiences, and perspectives. By breaking down the barriers that separate us, this dynamic mentorship can foster understanding, empathy, and collaboration, ultimately dismantling the enduring inequalities that plague our society.

For the younger generation, intergenerational mentorship provides a unique opportunity to tap into the wealth of experience and wisdom that their elders possess. The guidance and support offered by seasoned mentors can help young people navigate the challenges they face, both personally and professionally. Mentorship empowers them to develop critical skills, make informed decisions, and cultivate resilience in the face of adversity.

Equally important, intergenerational mentorship offers older individuals a chance to stay connected, engaged, and relevant. It provides a sense of purpose and fulfillment that comes from sharing their accumulated knowledge and life lessons with those who will carry the torch forward. By actively participating in the growth and development of younger generations, older mentors can find renewed energy and a renewed sense of purpose.

Moreover, intergenerational mentorship has the potential to address the enduring inequalities that exist in our society. By fostering understanding and empathy between different generations, we can break free from the confines of age-based stereotypes and biases. This creates an environment where everyone's unique strengths and perspectives are valued, irrespective of their age. By collectively fighting against inequality, we can build a more inclusive and harmonious society for all.

To the youth, intergenerational mentorship offers a message of hope and possibility. It encourages them to seek out mentors, both young and old, who can guide and support them on their journey. It reminds them that they are not alone in their fight against inequality, and that they have the power to rise above the curtain that separates us.

In conclusion, intergenerational mentorship is a powerful tool that can empower individuals of all ages to fight inequality. By embracing the wisdom and experiences of older generations, while also valuing the fresh perspectives and innovative ideas of the youth, we can create a society that thrives on collaboration and mutual respect. Let us tear down the curtain that separates us and together, build a more equitable and inclusive world.

COLLABORATIVE SOLUTIONS FOR INEQUALITY

In a world plagued by enduring inequalities and the societal curtain that divides us, it is essential for individuals of all ages to come together and find collaborative solutions. This subchapter, titled "Collaborative Solutions for Inequality," aims to empower readers of all demographics to rise above the curtain and actively fight against the injustices that persist in our society.

Inequality is a complex issue that affects individuals from all walks of life. It encompasses disparities in income, education, healthcare, and opportunities. However, by working collaboratively, we can dismantle the barriers that perpetuate these inequalities and create a more equitable future for all.

One of the key messages addressed in this subchapter is the importance of engaging the youth in the fight against inequality. The youth are the future leaders and change-makers of our society, and it is crucial to provide them with the tools, knowledge, and inspiration to challenge and overcome the barriers that divide us. By empowering the youth, we can foster a sense of collective responsibility towards creating a more just and inclusive world.

This subchapter explores various collaborative solutions that can be implemented to combat inequality. It emphasizes the significance of education as a catalyst for change. By promoting equal access to quality education, we can equip individuals with the skills and knowledge needed to break free from the cycle of poverty and inequality.

Additionally, it highlights the importance of mentorship programs, where individuals from different backgrounds can come together to inspire and support one another.

Furthermore, this subchapter delves into the power of community engagement and grassroots movements. By mobilizing communities, we can amplify our collective voices and demand systemic changes that address the root causes of inequality. It displays inspiring stories of individuals who have successfully initiated change through community organizing and collective action.

"Collaborative Solutions for Inequality" serves as a call to action for readers of all ages, urging them to rise above the curtain and actively contribute to the fight against inequality. By working together, we can dismantle the societal barriers that divide us and create a world where everyone, regardless of their background, has equal opportunities to thrive. Let this subchapter inspire you to join the movement, empower the youth, and create a more just and inclusive society for all.

EMPOWERING ALL AGES THROUGH MUTUAL SUPPORT

In a society plagued by enduring inequalities, it is crucial to recognize the power of mutual support in empowering individuals of all ages. In this subchapter, we will explore how fostering connections and solidarity among different age groups can help dismantle the curtain that separates us and inspire meaningful

The Curtain That Divides US: A metaphor for society's Perpetual Inequalities.
Message for the youths

change. This message is particularly relevant to the youths, who hold the potential to shape a more egalitarian future.

Mutual support transcends age boundaries, recognizing that every individual, regardless of their age, possesses unique experiences, perspectives, and strengths. By harnessing these diverse qualities, we can forge a powerful alliance against inequality. It is essential to create spaces where people of all ages can come together to share their stories, struggles, and hopes. Through this exchange, we can build empathy, foster understanding, and develop collective solutions to address the deep-rooted disparities in our society.

To empower all ages, we must prioritize intergenerational collaboration. By bridging the gap between young and old, we can tap into the wisdom of the older generation while benefiting from the fresh ideas and energy of the youth. This collaboration can take various forms, such as mentorship programs, intergenerational dialogue sessions, or joint community projects. By working together, we can learn from one another, challenge stereotypes, and break down the barriers that perpetuate inequality.

Furthermore, empowering all ages requires active efforts to ensure equal access to resources and opportunities. It is our responsibility to create an inclusive society where age does not determine one's worth or potential. This means advocating for affordable education, healthcare, and social services for all age groups. It also entails challenging ageism and age-based discrimination in employment and other spheres of life. When we value and invest in individuals of all ages, we create a society where everyone has the opportunity to thrive.

For the youths, this message is particularly pertinent. They are the torchbearers of change, the ones who will shape the future. By embracing the power of mutual support and intergenerational collaboration, they can break free from the limitations imposed by the curtain of inequality. They have the ability to challenge societal norms, demand justice, and create a more equitable world.

In conclusion, empowering all ages through mutual support is a powerful tool in dismantling the enduring inequalities in our society. By fostering connections and collaboration among different age groups, we can break down the barriers that separate us and work towards a more inclusive future. This message is particularly meaningful for the youths, who hold the key to transforming our society. Let us unite, support one another, and rise above the curtain of inequality, creating a world where all ages can thrive.

CELEBRATING PROGRESS AND INSPIRING HOPE

In a world where enduring inequalities continue to divide societies, it is essential to pause and appreciate the progress we have made while also inspiring hope for a better future. This subchapter, titled "Celebrating Progress and Inspiring Hope," aims to empower individuals of all ages and shed light on the curtain that separates us, particularly addressing the youth who hold the key to shaping a more equal society.

It is crucial to acknowledge the milestones we have achieved in the quest for equality. Throughout history, incredible advancements have been made, from the abolition of slavery to the fight for women's suffrage and civil rights movements. These triumphs should serve as a reminder that change is possible, and with determination, we can overcome the barriers that divide us.

However, it is equally important to recognize that inequalities persist in our society. The curtain that divides us still exists, manifesting in various forms such as economic disparities, racial discrimination, and gender inequality. By highlighting these enduring challenges, we can foster a sense of urgency and build collective determination to address them head-on.

To inspire hope, we must highlight the remarkable stories of individuals who have risen above the curtain of inequality. These stories, regardless of age or background, serve as beacons of inspiration for all. From activists who have fought tirelessly for social justice to everyday heroes who have dedicated their lives to uplifting others, their stories remind us of the power we possess to effect change.

For the youth, this subchapter provides a message of empowerment and encourages them to become agents of change. It emphasizes the importance of education, empathy, and engagement in dismantling the barriers that perpetuate inequality. By nurturing their passion, providing them with knowledge, and creating platforms for their voices to be heard, we can equip the youth with the tools they need to shape a more equitable future.

"Celebrating Progress and Inspiring Hope" serves as a call to action for all ages. It invites individuals to reflect on the progress we have made, recognize the work that remains, and unite in a shared vision of equality. By celebrating the victories, learning from the past, and empowering the youth, we can collectively rise above the curtain that separates us and build a more just and inclusive society for all.

RECOGNIZING POSITIVE CHANGE AND ACHIEVEMENTS

In our journey towards fighting inequality and breaking down the curtain that separates us, it is important to not only acknowledge the enduring inequalities in society but also celebrate the positive change and achievements that have been made along the way.

This subchapter aims to inspire and empower individuals of all ages, particularly the youth, by highlighting the progress that has been achieved and the individuals who have played a vital role in bringing about positive change.

Throughout history, there have been countless instances where individuals and communities have risen above adversity and fought against inequality. From civil rights movements to gender equality campaigns, the efforts of these courageous individuals have paved the way for a fairer and more inclusive society. It is crucial to recognize and celebrate these achievements as they demonstrate the power of collective action and remind us that change is possible.

The Curtain That Divides US: A metaphor for society's Perpetual Inequalities.
Message for the youths

One remarkable example of positive change is the civil rights movement in the United States, led by influential figures like Martin Luther King Jr. and Rosa Parks. Their unwavering determination and commitment to equality not only challenged the injustices of racial segregation but also inspired millions around the world to stand up against discrimination in all its forms. Their efforts led to the passage of landmark legislation, such as the Civil Rights Act of 1964, which outlawed discrimination based on race, color, religion, sex, or national origin.

In the realm of gender equality, we have witnessed significant progress as well. Women's suffrage movements fought tirelessly for the right to vote, ultimately leading to the enfranchisement of women in many countries. Today, women continue to break barriers and excel in various fields, be it politics, science, or business. Their achievements serve as a reminder that gender should never limit one's potential.

Recognizing positive change and achievements is not only about celebrating historical milestones but also acknowledging the everyday heroes who work tirelessly to make a difference in their communities. Whether it is a teacher who inspires and uplifts their students, a social worker who fights for the rights of the marginalized, or a young activist using their voice to raise awareness, these individuals play a vital role in creating a more equitable society.

or the youth, recognizing positive change and achievements serves as a source of inspiration and motivation. By highlighting the achievements of those who came before them, they can see that their actions have the potential to bring about meaningful change. It empowers them to use their voices, talents, and passions to fight against inequality and build a better future for all.

In conclusion, recognizing positive change and achievements is an essential part of our journey towards fighting inequality. By celebrating the progress that has been made and highlighting the individuals who have played a role in bringing about change, we can inspire and empower people of all ages, particularly the youth, to continue the fight for a more just and inclusive society.

INSPIRING INDIVIDUALS AND COMMUNITIES TO TAKE ACTION

In a world plagued by enduring inequalities, it is crucial to inspire individuals and communities of all ages to rise above the curtain and take action. In this subchapter, we will explore the power of collective action and how it can empower people to fight against inequality.

The curtain that separates us symbolizes the barriers that divide societies - be it race, gender, socioeconomic status, or any other form of discrimination. These inequalities persist, hindering progress and social cohesion. However, the youth holds the key to dismantling these barriers and creating a more equitable future for all.

One of the most powerful tools in inspiring individuals and communities is education. By providing accessible and inclusive education, we can equip young minds with the knowledge and understanding necessary to challenge the status quo. Education empowers individuals to think critically, question social norms, and advocate for change. It is through education that we can inspire a new generation of activists and leaders.

Furthermore, storytelling plays a crucial role in inspiring action. Sharing the stories of individuals who have triumphed over adversity and fought against inequality can ignite a spark within others. These stories serve as a reminder that change is possible and that every individual has the power to make a difference. By highlighting these narratives, we can inspire individuals of all ages to take action and contribute to the greater good.

In addition to education and storytelling, fostering a sense of community is essential. When individuals come together, they can amplify their voices and create lasting change. Encouraging dialogue, organizing community events, and facilitating collaboration can ignite a sense of unity and purpose. By creating spaces for individuals to connect and share their experiences, we can inspire collective action and empower communities to address the inequalities that affect them.

Finally, it is crucial to provide tools and resources for individuals and communities to take action effectively. This can include organizing workshops, providing mentorship programs, or connecting them with organizations that align with their goals. By equipping individuals with the necessary tools and support, we can empower them to navigate the challenges they may face and create sustainable change.

In conclusion, inspiring individuals and communities of all ages to take action is crucial in the fight against enduring inequalities. By providing education, sharing inspiring stories, fostering a sense of community, and providing tools for action, we can empower individuals to rise above the curtain and create a more equitable society. The power lies within each and every one of us to challenge the status quo and build a future where equality is not just a dream but a reality for all.

CONCLUSION: BREAKING THE CHAINS OF INEQUALITY: OUR COLLECTIVE RESPONSIBILITY

In a world plagued by inequality, it is our collective responsibility to rise above the barriers that divide us and fight for a society where every individual, regardless of age, is empowered and given equal opportunities. Throughout this book, "The Curtain that Divides Us: A Metaphor for Society's Perpetual Inequalities. A Message for the Youths," we have explored the enduring inequalities that persist in our society and discussed the message we must convey to the youths who will shape our future.

Inequality exists in various forms, whether it be economic, educational, or social. It is a curtain that divides us, hindering progress and perpetuating a cycle of disadvantage for certain groups. However, we must remember that this curtain is not impenetrable. It is within our power to dismantle it and create a more inclusive and just society.

We have seen that the fight against inequality knows no age boundaries. Young or old, we all have a role to play in breaking these chains. For the youths, this message is particularly critical. They are the torchbearers of change, the ones who will inherit the world we leave behind. It is our duty to empower them with knowledge, resilience, and the tools they need to challenge injustice and build a fairer future.

Empowering the youth starts with education and awareness. We must teach them about the inequalities that persist and help them understand the root causes. By fostering empathy and understanding, we can inspire them to take action and become advocates for change. We must encourage them to question the status quo, challenge stereotypes, and stand up against discrimination in all its forms.

Additionally, it is essential to provide equal opportunities for all ages. By investing in quality education and accessible healthcare, we can level the playing field and ensure that no one is left behind. We must also create spaces for intergenerational dialogue and collaboration, fostering a sense of unity and collective responsibility.

In conclusion, breaking the chains of inequality requires a united effort from individuals of all ages. It is our collective responsibility to fight against the enduring inequalities in society and empower the youth to become agents of change. By working together, we can tear down the curtain that divides us and build a future where every individual, regardless of their age, has an equal chance to thrive. Let us rise above the barriers and create a society that values and uplifts all its members.

The Curtain That Divides US: A metaphor for society's Perpetual Inequalities.
Message for the youths

SECTION II –

THE COST OF INEQUALITY: EXAMINING RACIAL WAGE GAPS IN HEALTHCARE, FINANCE, AND TECHNOLOGY

The Curtain That Divides US: A metaphor for society's Perpetual Inequalities.
Message for the youths

INTRODUCTION: SIGNIFICANCE OF WAGE DISPARITIES

This section contains an overview of the crucial issue of wage disparities within specific industries, with a particular focus on examining the wage gaps between Black and white workers. Wage disparities have long plagued various sectors, including healthcare, finance, and technology. Despite advancements in civil rights and diversity initiatives, Black workers continue to experience significant wage gaps compared to their white counterparts. This subsection aims to shed light on the background and significance of these disparities, providing a comprehensive understanding of the factors contributing to inequities in wages; exploring the underlying reasons behind these disparities, and addressing both structural and statistical factors that contribute to wage gaps.

One important source supporting this analysis is the research conducted by Kale and Chandra in their article "Racial Wage Gaps in Medicine: Structural, Statistical, and Ethical Considerations" (2020). This study illustrates how structural barriers within the healthcare industry, such as discriminatory hiring practices and limited access to educational opportunities, contribute to wage disparities between black and white healthcare professionals. By understanding these structural factors, we can gain insights into the systemic issues that perpetuate wage gaps.

Additionally, the research conducted by Khatiwada et al. in their article "Racial and Ethnic Wage Gaps in the California Health Care Sector" (2018) provides valuable Insights into the significance of wage disparities in the healthcare sector specifically. This study highlights the urgent need to address these gaps to improve the quality of healthcare provided to minority populations and ensure fair compensation for black professionals in the industry.

By examining wage disparities in healthcare, finance, and technology, we can gain a comprehensive understanding of the challenges faced by Black workers in these sectors. And further explore the implications of wage gaps on individuals, families, and communities, underscoring the need for equitable compensation and opportunities for advancement. Through a combination of statistical data, personal anecdotes, and industry insights, the aim is to empower minority readers to advocate for fair treatment and equal pay within their respective industries. The hope is to inspire dialogue and change, promoting a more inclusive and equitable workforce for all.

The goal is to explore and respond to an overarching

question, "What are the reasons behind the wage gaps between Black and white workers within sectors such as healthcare, finance, and technology?" This question underpins the examination of racial wage gaps in healthcare, finance, and technology. Specifically geared towards minorities, particularly the Black community, this section aims to shed light on the wage disparities within these specific industries and provide an understanding of the factors contributing to these gaps.

To answer this question, we will analyze the structural, statistical, and ethical considerations involved. Two sources guide the exploration for answers. The first source, "Racial Wage Gaps in Medicine: Structural, Statistical, and Ethical Considerations" by Kale and Chandra (2020), provides valuable insights into the racial wage gaps specifically within the healthcare sector. This source delves into the underlying structural factors perpetuating these gaps, such as discrimination, occupational segregation, and unequal access to opportunities for career advancement. The second source, "Racial and Ethnic Wage Gaps in the California Health Care Sector" by Khatiwada et al. (2018), focuses on the healthcare sector within a specific region. By examining the wage disparities in California, we aim to gain a localized understanding of the factors at play and identify any unique challenges faced by Black workers in this context.

By synthesizing the findings from these sources and conducting further research, the chapter covers the following:

1. An overview of the wage gaps between Black and white workers within the healthcare, finance, and technology sectors.

2. Identify the key factors contributing to these wage disparities, including but not limited to discrimination, occupational segregation, and limited access to career advancement opportunities.

3. An exploration of the potential consequences of these wage gaps on the overall socioeconomic well-being of Black workers.

4. Highlights any existing efforts or initiatives aimed at reducing these disparities and promoting equal pay within these industries.

5. Proposal of recommendations and strategies for policymakers, employers, and individuals to address and mitigate the racial wage gaps within healthcare, finance, and technology.

In conclusion, this approach delivers groundbreaking content that delves into the deep-rooted issue of wage disparities between Black and white workers within specific industries. And provides an overview of the research work on "The Cost of Inequality: Examining Racial Wage Gaps in Healthcare, Finance, and Technology," highlighting its purpose, key sources, and target audience. The aim is to shed light on the pervasive wage gaps that exist within sectors crucial to the economic growth and prosperity of our nation - healthcare, finance, and technology. Focusing specifically on the experiences of minorities, particularly Black people, we explore the structural, statistical, and ethical considerations that contribute to these disparities.

Minorities, particularly Black people, who have personally experienced or witnessed the unjust wage gaps within these industries will find this chapter meaningful. However, the aim is to empower them with knowledge and understanding, equipping them with the tools to advocate for change and bridge these disparities. Furthermore, this chapter will also be of interest to individuals and organizations invested in wage disparities within specific industries. Professionals in healthcare, finance, and technology who want to better understand the challenges faced by minority workers and explore strategies to address these gaps will find this section highly informative.

CHAPTER I: UNDERSTANDING WAGE DISPARITIES

DEFINITION AND MEASUREMENT OF WAGE GAPS

Wage gaps refer to the differences in earnings between different racial or ethnic groups, with a specific focus on the disparities between Black and white workers. These gaps can be measured using various approaches, including the raw wage gap and the adjusted wage gap. The raw wage gap compares the average earnings of Black and white workers without accounting for any other factors, such as education, experience, or occupation. On the other hand, the adjusted wage gap takes into consideration these factors to provide a more accurate assessment of the wage disparities. In their study on "Racial Wage Gaps in Medicine: Structural, Statistical, and Ethical Considerations", Kale and Chandra (2020) argue that racial wage gaps cannot be solely attributed to individual characteristics, but rather are influenced by systemic factors such as discrimination, occupational segregation, and limited access to resources and opportunities.

Another significant study by Khatiwada et al. (2018) titled

"Racial and Ethnic Wage Gaps in the California Health Care Sector" emphasizes the need to examine wage disparities within specific industries, such as healthcare. This research explores the wage gaps specifically within the healthcare sector in California and identifies the factors that contribute to these disparities, including occupational segregation, educational attainment, and discrimination. By examining these studies and others like them, provide a deeper understanding of the wage gaps between Black and white workers within specific industries. This knowledge is crucial for addressing and advocating for equal pay and opportunities for minorities, particularly within sectors such as healthcare, finance, and technology. By shedding light on the structural and systemic factors that contribute to these wage gaps, we can work towards implementing policies and practices that promote fairness, equity, and inclusivity within these industries.

The definition and measurement of wage gaps provide essential groundwork for understanding the extent and causes of disparities between Black and white workers within specific industries. The research by Kale and Chandra (2020) and Khatiwada et al. (2018) highlights the importance of examining structural factors and industry-specific wage gaps. By addressing these issues, we can strive towards creating a more equitable and inclusive workforce for minorities, promoting social justice and economic empowerment.

FACTORS CONTRIBUTING TO WAGE DISPARITIES

To address the issue of wage disparities between minority and white workers within specific industries such as healthcare, finance, and technology, it is important to understand the factors that contribute to these gaps. This subchapter aims to explore the various causes of wage disparities and shed light on the structural, statistical, and ethical considerations surrounding this issue.

Structural Factors

Structural factors play a significant role in perpetuating wage disparities. Historical racial discrimination, segregation, and unequal access to education and employment opportunities have created a system that disadvantages minority workers. Discrimination in hiring and promotion practices, as well as occupational segregation, where certain jobs are dominated by a particular race, further contribute to wage gaps.

Statistical Factors

Statistical factors also contribute to wage disparities. Studies have shown that Black workers are often concentrated in lower-paying jobs within specific industries. This occupational segregation leads to lower wages for Black workers compared to their white counterparts, who tend to occupy higher-paying positions. Furthermore, research has found that even when Black workers possess the same qualifications and experience as their white counterparts, they still face wage gaps, indicating the presence of discrimination.

Ethical Considerations

The issue of wage disparities raises ethical concerns that need to be addressed. Paying workers differently for doing the same job based on their race or ethnicity is unjust and promotes inequality. It undermines the principles of fairness and equal opportunity.

Wage disparities within specific industries, such as healthcare, finance, and technology, are influenced by various factors. Structural factors, including historical discrimination and occupational segregation, create an unequal playing field for minority workers. Statistical factors, such as job concentration and discrimination within hiring and promotion practices, further contribute to wage gaps. Additionally, the ethical considerations surrounding wage disparities highlight the importance of striving for equal pay regardless of race or ethnicity. By understanding these factors, we can work towards dismantling the barriers that perpetuate wage disparities and create a more equitable society for all workers.

HISTORICAL CONTEXT OF RACIAL WAGE GAPS

Understanding the historical context of racial wage gaps is crucial in comprehending the systemic inequalities that persist in various industries today. This subchapter aims to shed light on the factors that have contributed to wage disparities between Black and white workers across sectors such as healthcare, finance, and technology. By examining the historical roots of these gaps, we can begin to address the underlying issues and work towards creating a more equitable future.

Historically, racial wage gaps in healthcare, finance, and

technology have been deeply entrenched in discriminatory practices and policies. For centuries, Black individuals have faced systemic racism, which has limited their access to education, training, and employment opportunities. This exclusionary environment has perpetuated a cycle of economic disadvantage, leading to lower wages and limited upward mobility for Black workers compared to their white counterparts.

In the healthcare industry, studies such as "Racial Wage Gaps in Medicine: Structural, Statistical, and Ethical Considerations" by Kale and Chandra (2020) and "Racial and Ethnic Wage Gaps in the California Health Care Sector" by Khatiwada et al. (2018) have highlighted the persistent wage disparities faced by black healthcare professionals. These gaps can be traced back to historical factors such as racial segregation, unequal access to quality education, and discriminatory hiring practices. Additionally, implicit biases and stereotypes have played a role in perpetuating these wage gaps, with Black healthcare workers often being undervalued and undercompensated for their skills and contributions.

Similarly, in the finance and technology sectors, the historical context of racial wage gaps can be attributed to systemic racism and exclusionary practices. Black workers have historically faced barriers to entry and advancement in these industries, leading to limited representation and opportunities for career growth. Studies have shown that black professionals in finance and technology are often paid less than their white counterparts, even when controlling for factors such as education and experience.

Addressing these historical disparities requires a multi-faceted approach. It involves challenging and dismantling discriminatory hiring practices, promoting diversity and inclusion within organizations, and implementing policies that ensure fair compensation and advancement opportunities for all employees. Furthermore, bridging the educational and skills gap among minority communities is essential to provide equal access to training and employment opportunities within these industries.

The historical context of racial wage gaps in healthcare, finance, and technology reveals a deeply rooted system of discrimination and exclusion. By understanding these historical factors, we can begin to address the systemic inequalities that persist today. It is crucial for minorities, particularly Black individuals, to be aware of these historical injustices and advocate for change within their respective industries. Only through collective efforts can we strive toward a more equitable society, where everyone has an equal opportunity to succeed and thrive.

IMPACTS OF WAGE DISPARITIES ON MINORITIES

Wage disparities within specific industries, such as healthcare, finance, or technology, have long been concerning issues for minorities, particularly Black workers. This chapter sheds light on the profound impacts these disparities have on the lives and opportunities of minority individuals. Drawing on the research by Kale and Chandra (2020) and Khatiwada et al. (2018), this subchapter aims to provide an in-depth understanding of the consequences of wage disparities on minorities.

One of the most significant impacts of wage disparities on minorities is the perpetuation of economic inequality. The wage gaps between Black and white workers within specific sectors create a cycle of poverty and limited economic mobility for minority individuals. With lower wages, minorities often struggle to meet their basic needs, let alone build wealth or invest in their future. This economic disadvantage not only affects their present circumstances but also hinders their ability to improve their socio-economic status over time. Moreover, wage disparities have a profound impact on the overall health and well-being of minorities. Research has shown that lower wages are associated with increased stress levels, mental health issues, and limited access to quality healthcare. As minorities are more likely to experience wage disparities, they face higher rates of these negative health outcomes. This not only affects their personal lives but also places an added burden on the healthcare system, further exacerbating existing inequalities.

Furthermore, wage disparities within specific industries can lead to limited representation and opportunities for minorities. When Black workers are consistently paid less than their white counterparts, it perpetuates the underrepresentation of minorities in higher-paying positions. This lack of representation not only limits the career growth and advancement of minority individuals but also hinders the progress toward a more diverse and inclusive workforce.

The impacts of wage disparities on minorities, particularly Black workers, are far-reaching and detrimental. From perpetuating economic inequality and hindering socio-economic mobility to negatively impacting health outcomes and limiting opportunities for advancement, these disparities have a profound effect on the lives and well-being of minority individuals. Society, industries, and policymakers must address and rectify these disparities to create a more equitable and inclusive society.

CHAPTER II: WAGE DISPARITIES IN HEALTHCARE

OVERVIEW OF THE HEALTHCARE INDUSTRY

The healthcare industry plays a crucial role in society, providing essential medical services to individuals and communities. However, it is important to recognize that this industry, like many others, is not immune to the issue of wage disparities, particularly between Black and white workers. The healthcare industry encompasses a wide range of sectors, including hospitals, clinics, pharmaceutical companies, research institutions, and insurance providers. It employs millions of individuals, offering diverse career opportunities. However, despite the increasing diversity in the workforce, there are significant wage gaps that disproportionately affect minorities, particularly Black workers. Studies such as "Racial Wage Gaps in Medicine: Structural, Statistical, and Ethical Considerations" by Kale and Chandra (2020) and "Racial and Ethnic Wage Gaps in the California Health Care Sector" by Khatiwada et al. (2018) provide valuable insights into this issue. These sources highlight the structural, statistical, and ethical factors contributing to the wage disparities within the healthcare industry.

Structurally, the healthcare industry has historically been dominated by white professionals, which has perpetuated unequal opportunities for Black workers. This lack of representation at higher levels of leadership and decision-making positions has contributed to the persistence of wage gaps. Additionally, statistical analysis reveals that Black workers, even when holding similar positions and possessing similar qualifications, earn less than their white counterparts.

Ethically, the existence of racial wage gaps in the healthcare industry raises concerns about fairness and equity. It is essential to address these disparities to ensure equal access to opportunities and fair compensation for all workers, regardless of their racial or ethnic background. By examining the wage gaps within the healthcare industry, we can identify the specific challenges faced by Black workers and develop strategies to address these disparities. Through this knowledge, we can advocate for change and work towards a more equitable and inclusive healthcare industry for all individuals, irrespective of their race or ethnicity.

The healthcare industry, although vital to society, is not

exempt from wage disparities. The racial wage gaps that exist within this sector disproportionately affect Black workers. It is imperative to explore the factors contributing to these gaps and work towards creating a more equitable and inclusive environment within the healthcare industry. Only by understanding and addressing these disparities can we strive for a fairer future for all individuals, regardless of their racial or ethnic background.

RACIAL WAGE GAPS IN HEALTHCARE: STATISTICS AND TRENDS

In the ongoing battle against racial inequality, one area that demands our attention is the persistent wage gaps within specific industries. For minorities, particularly Black people, it is crucial to understand the extent of these disparities within sectors like healthcare, finance, and technology. This subsection focuses on the healthcare industry, shedding light on the statistics and trends surrounding racial wage gaps. Studies by Kale and Chandra (2020) and by Khatiwada et al. (2018), show that the wage gap between black and white healthcare professionals remains substantial, even after controlling for factors such as education, experience, and occupation. These findings highlight the structural and systemic factors contributing to the perpetuation of inequality within the industry.

Trends in Racial Wage Gaps

Examining the trends over time, Khatiwada et al. (2018) found that racial wage gaps in the healthcare sector have not significantly narrowed in recent years. Despite advancements in diversity and inclusion efforts, the wage disparities persist, pointing to the need for further examination and action. These trends emphasize the importance of addressing the root causes of inequality, rather than relying solely on superficial diversity initiatives.

Factors Influencing Racial Wage Gaps

Research suggests that a combination of factors, including occupational segregation, discrimination, and limited access to educational opportunities, play a significant role in perpetuating the wage gaps. By recognizing these factors, we can work towards implementing targeted interventions and policies that address the root causes of inequality.

The statistics and trends surrounding racial wage gaps in

healthcare paint a concerning picture for minorities, particularly blacks. Despite progress made in various domains, the wage disparities within the healthcare sector remain substantial. Understanding the factors influencing these gaps is crucial in developing effective strategies to combat inequality. By examining the research presented in this subsection, we hope to empower minorities, particularly Black workers, and youths, by equipping them with knowledge and awareness to advocate for fair wages and equal opportunities within the healthcare industry. Together, we can strive to dismantle the barriers that hinder progress and create a more inclusive and equitable future.

FACTORS AFFECTING WAGE DISPARITIES IN HEALTHCARE

In this subsection, we examine the factors that contribute to wage disparities within the healthcare industry, specifically focusing on the wage gaps between Black and white workers. Drawing on recent research studies by Kale and Chandra (2020), Khatiwada et al. (2018 and expert opinions, we aim to shed light on the structural, statistical, and ethical considerations that underlie these disparities.

Structural Factors

One prominent factor that contributes to wage disparities in healthcare is occupational segregation. Black workers tend to be concentrated in lower-paying positions such as nursing assistants or medical technicians, while white workers occupy higher-paying roles like physicians or surgeons. This occupational segregation is influenced by historical and social factors, perpetuating the inequality in wages.

Statistical Factors

Research shows that even when Black workers hold similar positions and possess comparable qualifications to their white counterparts, they still experience wage disparities. This phenomenon, known as the unexplained wage gap, suggests the presence of systemic biases and discrimination within the healthcare industry. Factors such as unconscious bias during the hiring process, unequal access to training and promotions, and limited networking opportunities contribute to this statistical disparity.

Ethical Considerations

The presence of wage disparities in healthcare raises ethical concerns. It undermines the principles of fairness and equal opportunity for all workers, irrespective of their race or ethnicity. The perpetuation of such disparities not only impacts the financial well-being of Black workers but also hinders career advancement opportunities, leading to limited representation of minorities in leadership positions within the healthcare industry.

Wage disparities within the healthcare industry, specifically between Black and white workers, are influenced by a combination of structural, statistical, and ethical factors.

Occupational segregation, systemic biases, and limited access to training and promotions all contribute to these disparities. Policymakers, healthcare institutions, and stakeholders need to recognize these factors and work towards implementing measures to address and eliminate wage gaps. By promoting diversity, equity, and inclusion, we can create a healthcare system that values and rewards all workers equally, regardless of their racial or ethnic background.

CASE STUDY: EXAMINING RACIAL WAGE GAPS IN MEDICINE

In the quest to understand and address the pervasive issue of racial wage gaps within specific industries, it is crucial to turn our attention to the field of medicine. Healthcare, often regarded as a noble profession, is unfortunately not immune to the systemic disparities that exist in our society. In this subsection, we will review the research and evidence surrounding racial wage gaps in medicine, shedding light on the structural, statistical, and ethical considerations that perpetuate this injustice.

The study by Kale and Chandra (2020) offers a comprehensive analysis of the racial disparities within the healthcare sector. The research highlights the alarming wage gaps between Black and white workers, revealing an undeniable and deeply ingrained bias that affects the earning potential of black healthcare professionals. The study serves as a wake-up call, urging us to critically examine the underlying factors contributing to these disparities.

Additionally, the study conducted by Khatiwada et al. (2018) offers valuable insights specific to the state of California. The research underscores the persistent wage gaps experienced by minorities within the healthcare industry, further emphasizing the urgent need for systemic change.

The examination of these studies highlights the urgency to address the racial wage gaps in medicine. It is essential to acknowledge the structural barriers that hinder career advancement and equal pay for black healthcare professionals. Factors such as bias in hiring and promotion practices, lack of diversity in leadership positions, and unequal access to educational and training opportunities contribute to the perpetuation of these disparities. Furthermore, it is crucial to consider the ethical implications of these wage gaps. Not only do they impact the financial stability and livelihoods of black healthcare professionals, but they also perpetuate a cycle of inequality that affects the quality of healthcare provided to marginalized communities. By failing to value and compensate black professionals fairly, we undermine the trust and rapport between healthcare providers and patients, ultimately hindering the progress toward equitable healthcare outcomes for all.

In summary, this case study of racial wage gaps in medicine shed light on the structural, statistical, and ethical considerations that perpetuate this issue. The studies conducted by Kale and Chandra (2020) and Khatiwada et al. (2018) highlight the urgent need for systemic change within the healthcare industry. By addressing the underlying factors contributing to these disparities, we can strive towards a more equitable and inclusive healthcare system that values and compensates all professionals regardless of their race or ethnicity.

ETHICAL CONSIDERATIONS IN ADDRESSING HEALTHCARE WAGE DISPARITIES

Let us examine the ethical considerations surrounding healthcare wage disparities faced by minorities, particularly Black individuals, within the healthcare industry. By exploring the research conducted by experts in the field, such as Kale, Chandra, Khatiwada, and others, we can gain a deeper understanding of the structural, statistical, and ethical factors that contribute to these disparities.

The healthcare industry plays a fundamental role in promoting well-being and addressing health inequalities. However, it is disheartening to discover that wage gaps persist within this sector, with Black workers consistently earning less than their white counterparts.

The Curtain That Divides US: A metaphor for society's Perpetual Inequalities.
Message for the youths

One important aspect to consider is the structural barriers that perpetuate wage disparities. Historical factors, such as discrimination and unequal access to education and advancement opportunities, have contributed to the unequal distribution of resources within the healthcare industry.

By acknowledging and confronting these structural barriers, we can begin to dismantle the systems that perpetuate wage disparities and create a more equitable healthcare workforce. Furthermore, statistical analysis plays a crucial role in identifying and quantifying the extent of wage gaps. Research studies, such as those conducted by Kale, Chandra, Khatiwada, and others, provide valuable insights into the magnitude of these disparities.

By examining the data, we can better understand the factors influencing wage gaps and develop targeted strategies to address them. However, it is not enough to rely solely on structural and statistical analyses. Ethical considerations play a vital role in guiding our actions and decisions. It is essential to recognize the inherent value and dignity of every individual, irrespective of their race or ethnicity. By addressing healthcare wage disparities, we are not only promoting fairness and justice, but we are also ensuring that all individuals have equal opportunities to thrive in their chosen professions.

CHAPTER III: WAGE DISPARITIES IN FINANCE

OVERVIEW OF THE FINANCE INDUSTRY

The finance industry plays a significant role in our economy, offering various career opportunities and contributing to the overall growth and development of businesses. However, when examining wage disparities in the finance industry, it is crucial to acknowledge the racial wage gaps that exist between Black and white workers. This section aims to provide an overview of the finance industry while shedding light on the racial wage gaps within this sector.

The finance industry encompasses a wide range of activities, including banking, investment management, insurance, and financial planning. It is a vital sector that facilitates the flow of capital, promotes economic stability, and supports individuals and businesses in achieving their financial goals. Within this industry, there are numerous roles and positions, ranging from entry-level positions to executive-level positions, each with varying levels of compensation.

However, studies have shown that Black workers within the finance industry face significant wage disparities compared to their white counterparts. Research by Kale and Chandra (2020) highlights the structural, statistical, and ethical considerations contributing to racial wage gaps in medicine, a sub-sector of the finance industry. Similarly, Khatiwada et al. (2018) examine the racial and ethnic wage gaps within the California healthcare sector, which intersects with finance. These studies and others provide valuable insights into the factors that contribute to the wage gaps within the finance industry.

Factors such as discriminatory hiring practices, lack of representation in leadership roles, and systemic biases can all play a role in perpetuating these disparities. Understanding these factors is critical in addressing and rectifying the wage gaps within the industry. By examining the wage disparities within the finance industry, we can identify areas that require attention and advocate for change. Initiatives that promote equal access to education and training, increase diversity in leadership positions, and enforce anti-discrimination policies are crucial steps in narrowing the wage gaps. Furthermore, individuals within the industry need to be aware of their rights, negotiate fair compensation, and hold their employers accountable for any discriminatory practices.

The finance industry offers numerous opportunities for career growth and economic advancement. However, it is important to acknowledge and address the racial wage gaps that exist within this sector. By understanding the factors contributing to these disparities and advocating for change, we can work towards creating a more inclusive and equitable finance industry for all individuals, regardless of their race or ethnicity.

RACIAL WAGE GAPS IN FINANCE: STATISTICS AND TRENDS

Research studies by Kale and Chandra (2020) and by Khatiwada et al. (2018), although focused on the healthcare sector, provide valuable insights that can be extrapolated to the finance industry as well. According to these studies, Black workers in the finance sector experience significant wage gaps when compared to their white counterparts. On average, Black workers earn considerably less than their white colleagues, even when factors such as education, experience, and job position are taken into account. These statistics point to systemic issues that need to be addressed to ensure a fair and equitable workplace for all.

Trends: The statistics indicate that several underlying trends are contributing to the racial wage gaps within the finance industry. One key trend is the lack of representation and inclusion of minorities in higher positions. Black professionals often face barriers in accessing senior management roles and executive positions, which significantly impacts their earning potential. This lack of representation also perpetuates a cycle of limited opportunities for career advancement. Another trend is the unconscious bias that exists within the finance industry. Studies have shown that biases, both explicit and implicit, affect the evaluation and compensation of Black workers. These biases can lead to lower starting salaries, slower salary growth, and limited access to bonuses and promotions.

The statistics and trends outlined in this section highlight the existence of racial wage gaps within the finance industry. These disparities are not only detrimental to the affected individuals but also hinder the overall progress towards a more inclusive and equitable society. Organizations within the finance sector need to acknowledge and address these disparities by implementing policies that promote diversity, inclusion, and equal pay. By doing so, they can create a more just and prosperous environment for all workers, regardless of their racial background.

FACTORS AFFECTING WAGE DISPARITIES IN FINANCE

In the field of finance, wage disparities between Black and white workers persist, highlighting the need for a deeper understanding of the factors contributing to this inequality. By examining the sources cited, Kale and Chandra (2020) and Khatiwada et al. (2018), we gain insight into the specific factors influencing wage disparities within the finance industry.

One of the key factors affecting wage disparities in finance is educational attainment. Historically, minorities, including Black people, have faced significant barriers to accessing quality education. This lack of educational opportunities can limit their ability to acquire the necessary skills and qualifications required for high-paying positions in finance. Additionally, systemic biases within educational systems can contribute to disparities in educational outcomes, perpetuating wage gaps between Black and white workers.

Another factor influencing wage disparities in finance is occupational segregation. Research has shown that Black workers are often concentrated in lower-paying positions within the industry, such as customer service or administrative roles, while their white counterparts tend to occupy higher-paying managerial or executive positions.

This occupational segregation can be attributed to various factors, including discrimination in hiring practices and limited access to professional networks and advancement opportunities. Discrimination and unconscious bias also play a significant role in perpetuating wage disparities in finance. Despite advancements in diversity and inclusion initiatives, Black workers still face discrimination in the workplace. Biases in performance evaluations, promotions, and salary negotiations can contribute to unequal pay for equal work.

Furthermore, the lack of diverse leadership within the finance industry can perpetuate these biases and hinder the advancement of black professionals. Government policies and regulations, or the lack thereof, also impact wage disparities in finance. The absence of robust anti-discrimination laws and weak enforcement mechanisms can allow discriminatory practices to persist. Additionally, the absence of transparent salary structures and pay equity initiatives can contribute to wage gaps within the industry.

To address wage disparities in finance, it is crucial to implement comprehensive strategies that address these underlying factors. These may include increasing access to quality education and training programs, promoting diversity and inclusion initiatives within the industry, enforcing anti-discrimination laws, and implementing pay equity measures. By addressing these factors, we can work towards creating a more equitable and inclusive finance industry for all workers, regardless of their race or ethnicity.

CASE STUDY: EXAMINING RACIAL WAGE GAPS IN THE CALIFORNIA HEALTH CARE SECTOR

In the United States, racial wage gaps persist across various industries, including healthcare. This section delves into an important case study that focuses on the California healthcare sector, shedding light on the disparities in wages between Black and white workers. By examining this specific industry, we aim to provide minorities, particularly Black people, with a deeper understanding of the challenges they face and the potential solutions to combat these inequalities.

The case study draws upon two significant sources: "Racial Wage Gaps in Medicine: Structural, Statistical, and Ethical Considerations" by Kale and Chandra (2020), and "Racial and Ethnic Wage Gaps in the California Health Care Sector" by Khatiwada et al. (2018). These studies highlight several key findings:

Persistent Wage Disparities

Despite advancements in civil rights and equal opportunity legislation, racial wage gaps continue to exist in the California healthcare sector. Black workers consistently earn lower wages compared to their white counterparts, even when controlling for factors such as education, experience, and job responsibilities.

Structural Factors

The case study reveals that structural factors, such as occupational segregation and discrimination, contribute significantly to the wage gaps. Black workers often find themselves concentrated in lower-paying positions within the healthcare sector, limiting their opportunities for career advancement and higher wages.

Statistical Analysis

The studies employ sophisticated statistical models to demonstrate that racial wage disparities cannot be solely attributed to individual characteristics. They show that even after accounting for various factors, a significant portion of the wage gaps remains unexplained, suggesting the presence of discrimination and bias.

Ethical Considerations

The case study explores the ethical implications of racial wage gaps, emphasizing the importance of addressing these disparities to promote social justice and equality. It highlights the need for healthcare organizations to adopt equitable policies and practices that ensure fair compensation for all workers, regardless of their race or ethnicity.

The case study on racial wage gaps in the California healthcare sector provides valuable insights into the challenges faced by minority workers, particularly Black people. By examining the structural, statistical, and ethical aspects of these wage disparities, it highlights the need for proactive measures to address and eliminate these inequities. As minorities seek equal opportunities and fair wages within specific industries, such as healthcare, finance, or technology, this case study serves as a call to action for both policymakers and industry leaders to champion diversity, inclusion, and pay equity. Only through collective efforts can we strive towards a more just society, where all individuals, regardless of their race, have equal access to opportunities and fair compensation.

STRATEGIES FOR REDUCING WAGE DISPARITIES IN FINANCE

Wage disparities between Black and white workers within the finance sector remain a pressing issue, hindering equal opportunities and economic advancement. This section will explore strategies for reducing wage disparities in finance, focusing on empowering minorities, particularly Black professionals, to bridge the racial wage gap. By examining existing research and insights from industry experts, we can identify effective strategies that can lead to a more equitable financial landscape.

Promoting Diversity and Inclusion Initiatives

Finance organizations must implement robust diversity and inclusion initiatives that prioritize representation at all levels of the hierarchy. This includes actively recruiting and retaining Black talent, creating mentorship programs, and establishing affinity groups. By fostering an inclusive environment, companies can counteract unconscious biases and promote equal opportunities for career advancement.

Salary Transparency and Pay Equity

Implementing salary transparency measures can help identify and address wage disparities. Companies should conduct regular pay audits to assess any wage gaps and take corrective actions to ensure pay equity. Establishing clear guidelines and standardized compensation practices can help eliminate bias in salary negotiations and promotions, providing a fair playing field for all employees.

Education and Skill Enhancement Programs

Providing targeted education and skill enhancement programs can empower black professionals to excel in the finance sector. These programs can include financial literacy workshops, mentoring programs, and access to industry certifications. Encouraging ongoing professional development can enhance career prospects and increase earning potential, ultimately reducing wage disparities.

Collaboration with Academic Institutions

Finance organizations should establish partnerships with academic institutions, particularly historically Black colleges, and universities, to facilitate internship and recruitment programs. By building strong relationships with these institutions, companies can tap into a diverse talent pool and provide opportunities for Black students to enter the finance industry.

Industry Advocacy and Policy Reform

Collaboration with industry associations and policymakers is crucial for driving systemic change. Finance organizations should actively advocate for policies that address wage disparities and promote equal pay. Lobbying for legislative changes, such as strengthening anti-discrimination laws and increasing transparency in pay reporting, can help create an environment where wage disparities are actively addressed.

Reducing wage disparities in the finance sector requires promoting diversity and inclusion, ensuring pay equity, providing education and skill enhancement programs, collaborating with academic institutions, and advocating for policy reform. By implementing these strategies, we can create a more equitable financial landscape that offers equal opportunities for black professionals, fostering economic growth and social justice within the industry.

CHAPTER IV: WAGE DISPARITIES IN TECHNOLOGY

OVERVIEW OF THE TECHNOLOGY INDUSTRY

In today's society, the technology industry has become a dominant force, shaping the way we live, work, and interact with one another. From the development of smartphones to the rise of social media platforms, and artificial intelligence, technology has revolutionized the world we live in. However, as we delve deeper into the industry, it becomes evident that there are significant disparities in wages, particularly between Black and white workers.

The technology industry, often referred to as the tech sector, encompasses a wide range of businesses involved in the creation, development, and distribution of technological products and services. These include software development companies, hardware manufacturers, internet service providers, and social media platforms, among others. The industry is known for its rapid growth, high salaries, and innovative culture, making it an attractive field for many individuals.

However, despite the opportunities that the tech industry

offers, there are persistent wage disparities between Black and white workers. The studies by Kale and Chandra (2020) and Khatiwada et al. (2018) have highlighted these disparities within the healthcare and finance sectors. While there is a limited amount of research specifically focused on the technology industry, existing data suggests that similar wage gaps exist within this sector as well.

The reasons behind these wage gaps are complex and multifaceted. Structural barriers, such as lack of access to quality education and limited opportunities for advancement, contribute to the disparities. Additionally, unconscious bias and discrimination may play a role in perpetuating these wage gaps. It is crucial to acknowledge and address these issues to create a more equitable and inclusive tech industry.

By exploring the wage disparities within the technology industry, we can better understand the challenges faced by Black workers and minorities. This section examines the factors contributing to these wage gaps and propose potential strategies for reducing them. It will also highlight the importance of representation, mentorship, and support networks within the industry to empower Black workers and promote diversity.

The technology industry offers immense opportunities for

growth and innovation. However, it is essential to recognize the existing wage disparities that disproportionately affect Black workers and minorities. By addressing these disparities and promoting inclusivity and diversity within the industry, we can strive towards a more equitable future for all.

FACTORS AFFECTING WAGE DISPARITIES IN TECHNOLOGY

In recent years, the technology sector has become a driving force in our economy, offering numerous job opportunities and attractive compensation packages. However, it is essential to recognize that wage disparities exist within this industry, particularly between Black and white workers. Understanding the factors that contribute to these wage gaps is crucial for addressing and rectifying this issue. This subchapter explores the various factors affecting wage disparities in technology, while exploring the root causes of this inequality.

Discrimination and bias in the workplace also play a significant role in perpetuating wage disparities. Research has shown that Black workers often face discrimination in hiring, promotion, and salary negotiations, leading to lower wages compared to their white counterparts. Implementing policies and practices that promote fairness and equality, such as blind hiring processes and pay transparency, can help mitigate these biases and reduce wage disparities.

One significant factor contributing to wage disparities in technology is educational attainment. Research has shown that Black workers, on average, have lower levels of educational attainment compared to their white counterparts. This disparity in education can lead to differences in skills and qualifications, ultimately affecting the wages offered to black workers. To address this issue, it is crucial to invest in education and provide equal opportunities for minorities to access quality education and training programs in technology-related fields.

Another factor that influences wage disparities in technology is occupational segregation. Studies have found that Black workers are often concentrated in lower-paying positions within the technology sector, such as technical support or customer service roles. This occupational segregation limits their earning potential and contributes to the wage gap between Black and white workers. Encouraging diversity and inclusion within technology companies and promoting equal opportunities for career advancement can help address this issue.

Furthermore, systemic factors, such as historical and societal inequalities, contribute to wage disparities in technology. The legacy of racial discrimination and unequal access to resources and opportunities has created a disadvantage for black workers, impacting their earning potential in the technology sector. Developing targeted initiatives and programs that address these historical inequities and provide support and resources for Black workers can help bridge the wage gap. By examining the various factors affecting wage disparities in technology, we can begin to develop strategies and policies to address this issue. Technology companies, policymakers, and society as a whole need to recognize the importance of equal pay and equal opportunities for all workers, regardless of their race or ethnicity. By working together, we can create a more equitable and inclusive technology industry that benefits everyone.

CASE STUDY: EXAMINING RACIAL WAGE GAPS IN TECHNOLOGY

In this subchapter, we review the alarming disparity in wages between Black and white workers within the technology sector. By examining the existing literature and case studies, we aim to expose the factors contributing to this racial wage gap and explore potential solutions to address this systemic issue.

Understanding the Racial Wage Gap in Technology

The wage disparities within the technology industry have been studied extensively, revealing a noticeable disparity between Black and white workers. This racial wage gap persists despite educational qualifications and experience, indicating that systemic biases may be at play. To gain a comprehensive understanding, we will draw upon two key sources: "Racial Wage Gaps in Medicine: Structural, Statistical, and Ethical Considerations" by Kale and Chandra (2020) and "Racial and Ethnic Wage Gaps in the California Health Care Sector" by Khatiwada et al. (2018).

Factors Contributing to the Racial Wage Gap

The research by Kale and Chandra (2020) suggests that structural barriers, such as discrimination in hiring and promotion practices, contribute significantly to the racial wage gap. Additionally, implicit biases and lack of diversity within leadership positions may perpetuate wage disparities. Khatiwada et al. (2018) further highlight the influence of educational attainment, occupational segregation, and limited access to networks and opportunities for career advancement.

Case Studies and Real-Life Examples

This subchapter includes case studies that highlight the experiences of black professionals in the technology industry. These firsthand accounts shed light on the challenges faced by Black workers in terms of wage inequality, limited career progression, and unconscious biases within the workplace. By examining these real-life examples, we aim to create awareness and encourage dialogue about the racial wage gap in technology.

Addressing the Racial Wage Gap

To combat this issue, it is crucial to implement proactive measures that foster diversity and inclusion within the technology sector. Companies must prioritize diverse hiring practices, mentorship programs, and unconscious bias training. Additionally, advocating for transparent salary structures and promoting equitable access to career advancement opportunities can help bridge the racial wage gap.

The racial wage gap in the technology sector is a pressing issue that demands attention and action. By examining case studies and drawing upon relevant research, we can better understand the factors contributing to this disparity. Through proactive efforts to foster diversity and inclusion, we can pave the way toward a more equitable and inclusive technology industry, where no one is held back by the color of their skin.

PROMOTING DIVERSITY AND INCLUSION IN THE TECH SECTOR

In recent years, there has been a growing recognition of the need to address diversity and inclusion in the tech sector. This subchapter focuses specifically on the wage disparities between Black and white workers within the technology industry and explores how we can promote diversity and inclusion in this sector. The tech industry has long been plagued by a lack of diversity, with Black workers being disproportionately underrepresented. This has resulted in significant wage gaps between Black and white workers, with Black employees consistently earning less than their white counterparts. This issue not only perpetuates economic inequality but also hampers the overall growth and innovation within the industry.

To understand the extent of this problem, we turn to recent studies such as "Racial Wage Gaps in Medicine: Structural, Statistical, and Ethical Considerations" and "Racial and Ethnic Wage Gaps in the California Health Care Sector" by Khatiwada et al. (2018). These studies shed light on the systemic issues that contribute to the wage disparities faced by Black workers within the tech sector.

Drawing on the studies of Kale and Chandra (2020) and Khatiwada et al. (2018), one of the key factors contributing to these disparities is the lack of representation and inclusion at all levels of the industry. Companies need to actively recruit and hire Black employees, not just for entry-level positions, but also for leadership roles. This can be achieved through targeted outreach programs, partnerships with organizations that support minority talent, and the implementation of diversity quotas. Additionally, it is crucial to address the implicit biases that exist within the industry. Unconscious prejudices can affect hiring decisions, performance evaluations, and promotion opportunities. Companies should invest in diversity and inclusion training programs to educate employees about these biases and encourage a more inclusive work environment.

Furthermore, fostering a culture of inclusion requires creating safe spaces for marginalized employees to voice their concerns and ideas. Establishing employee resource groups and affinity networks can provide a supportive community for Black workers, helping to combat feelings of isolation and discrimination. Lastly, it is important to hold companies accountable for their diversity and inclusion efforts. Transparency in reporting wage data, diversity metrics, and progress towards diversity goals can help drive change and ensure that companies are actively working towards reducing wage gaps.

By promoting diversity and inclusion within the tech sector, we can begin to address the wage disparities faced by Black workers. This not only creates a fairer and more equitable industry but also fosters innovation and growth by tapping into a wider pool of talent and perspectives. Companies, industry leaders, and policymakers must come together and take concrete steps towards building a more inclusive future in technology.

CHAPTER V: POLICY AND INTERVENTIONS

EXISTING POLICIES AND INTERVENTIONS ADDRESSING WAGE DISPARITIES

In recent years, there has been growing recognition of the persistent wage disparities between Black and white workers within specific industries such as healthcare, finance, and technology. These disparities not only contribute to economic inequality but also perpetuate systemic racism. In response to this issue, various policies and interventions have been implemented to address and reduce wage gaps.

One notable policy that has been put in place is affirmative action. Affirmative action aims to promote equal opportunities for historically marginalized groups, including Black people, by implementing policies that prioritize diversity and inclusion in hiring and promotion practices. These policies encourage employers to actively consider qualified minority candidates, thus helping to close the wage gap. However, an aspect of the affirmative action which allowed the use of race-based preferences in college admissions was overturned by the US supreme Court.

The Curtain That Divides US: A metaphor for society's Perpetual Inequalities.
Message for the youths

The affirmative action was intended to promote diversity and address historical discrimination against underrepresented groups, such as African Americans and Hispanics. In 2023, the US Supreme Court issued a landmark ruling that overturned affirmative action policies at two prestigious universities: Harvard College and the University of North Carolina (UNC). The ruling was based on two lawsuits filed by Students for Fair Admissions (SFFA), a nonprofit organization that advocates for race-neutral admissions policies was a reversal of a lower court's rulings that had upheld Harvard's and UNC's affirmative action programs. The Supreme Court's ruling effectively ended affirmative action at US universities, unless Congress passes legislation to restore it, or the court revisits the issue in the future.

Another important intervention is the enforcement of anti-discrimination laws. These laws prohibit employers from discriminating against employees on the basis of race, including in matters related to wages and promotions. By holding employers accountable and providing legal recourse for victims of discrimination, these laws play a crucial role in combating wage disparities. Additionally, efforts have been made to increase transparency and accountability within industries. Some organizations have implemented salary transparency measures, requiring employers to disclose salary information to employees. This helps to shine light on wage disparities and enables workers to negotiate fairer compensation. Furthermore, there have been initiatives to improve access to education and training opportunities for minorities. By providing scholarships, mentorship programs, and career development resources, these interventions aim to equip Black individuals with the skills and qualifications needed to secure higher-paying jobs within industries where wage gaps persist.

Existing policies and interventions have been implemented to address wage disparities between Black and white workers within specific industries. Affirmative action, anti-discrimination laws, transparency measures, and educational initiatives are among the strategies employed to reduce wage gaps. However, sustained efforts and ongoing research are needed to ensure that these policies are improved and effectively dismantle systemic racism and create a more equitable society for all.

EVALUATING THE EFFECTIVENESS OF CURRENT INITIATIVES

In addressing the persistent issue of racial wage gaps, it is crucial to evaluate the effectiveness of current initiatives aimed at reducing disparities within specific industries such as healthcare, finance, and technology. By examining the outcomes of these initiatives, we can gain insights into the progress made and identify areas that require further attention.

The study that examines racial wage gaps in the healthcare sector is "Racial Wage Gaps in Medicine: Structural, Statistical, and Ethical Considerations" by Kale and Chandra (2020). This research highlights the structural barriers that contribute to wage disparities and emphasizes the need for systemic changes. It underscores the importance of increasing diversity in leadership positions and implementing policies that promote equal pay and career advancement opportunities for minority healthcare professionals. Similarly, "Racial and Ethnic Wage Gaps in the California Health Care Sector" by Khatiwada et al. (2018) provides valuable insights into the wage gaps within the healthcare industry in a specific geographical context. This study emphasizes the need for comprehensive policies that address the unique challenges faced by minority healthcare workers in California. It advocates for targeted interventions to improve access to education and training, enhance job stability, and reduce discrimination in the workplace.

While these studies contribute to our understanding of racial wage gaps in healthcare, it is essential to evaluate the impact of initiatives in other industries such as finance and technology. The experiences of minorities, particularly Black people, in these sectors are often marked by significant disparities in wages and opportunities for career progression. To comprehensively evaluate the effectiveness of current initiatives, it is necessary to gather data and research from diverse sources. By examining the outcomes of various programs and policies, we can identify successful interventions and determine the factors that contribute to their effectiveness. This evaluation will enable us to replicate and scale up successful initiatives while addressing the shortcomings of others.

Furthermore, it is essential to prioritize the voices and experiences of minorities, especially Black people, in this evaluation process. Their insights can provide valuable perspectives on the barriers they face and the potential solutions that could be implemented. Engaging with minority communities and organizations is crucial to ensure that initiatives are responsive to their needs and aspirations.

Evaluating the effectiveness of current initiatives aimed at reducing racial wage gaps within specific industries is essential in our journey towards a more equitable society. By examining research studies like those mentioned above and gathering data from diverse sources, we can identify successful interventions while addressing the unique challenges faced by minorities, particularly Black people, in healthcare, finance, and technology sectors. This evaluation process must prioritize the voices and experiences of minorities to ensure that initiatives are effective and responsive to their needs.

RECOMMENDATIONS FOR POLICY CHANGES

To address the persistent racial wage gaps within specific industries such as healthcare, finance, and technology, it is crucial to implement policy changes that promote equity and fairness. The following recommended policy changes that can help bridge the wage gaps between Black and white workers, with a specific focus on minorities.

Implement Pay Transparency Measures

One key policy change that can help address wage disparities is the implementation of pay transparency measures. This involves requiring employers to disclose salary ranges for specific positions and providing employees with information about their colleagues' salaries. By increasing transparency, employees can better negotiate their wages and employers are held accountable for any wage disparities based on race.

Strengthen Equal Pay Laws

Existing equal pay laws need to be strengthened and enforced rigorously. This includes ensuring that employers are prohibited from discriminating in wages based on race, gender, or any other protected characteristics. Additionally, penalties for non-compliance should be increased to deter employers from engaging in discriminatory practices.

Develop and Expand Mentoring and Training Programs

To address the underrepresentation of minorities in higher-paying positions, it is crucial to develop and expand mentoring and training programs. These programs should specifically target Black employees and provide them with the necessary skills and support to advance in their careers. By providing equal opportunities for professional growth, we can help reduce wage disparities within specific sectors.

Promote Diversity and Inclusion Initiatives

Companies and organizations should actively promote diversity and inclusion initiatives. This includes setting diversity goals, implementing recruitment and retention strategies that target minorities, and creating inclusive work environments. By fostering diverse and inclusive workplaces, we can ensure that Black employees have equal access to opportunities for advancement and fair compensation.

Conduct Regular Pay Equity Audits

Regular pay equity audits should be conducted to identify and address any wage disparities based on race. These audits should be conducted by independent third parties and should include a thorough analysis of compensation practices, job classifications, and promotion processes. By proactively identifying and rectifying wage gaps, organizations can demonstrate their commitment to fairness and equality.

Implementing these policy changes is essential to combatting racial wage gaps within specific industries. By promoting equity, transparency, and equal opportunities, we can create a more inclusive and just society where all individuals, regardless of their race, have access to fair wages and opportunities for professional growth.

PROMOTING EQUITY AND EQUALITY IN THE WORKPLACE

Wage disparities continue to persist, particularly for marginalized communities, including minorities and Black people. This subchapter aims to review the wage gaps within the healthcare, finance, and technology industries, and explore strategies for promoting equity and equality in the workplace.

Research conducted by Kale and Chandra (2020) highlights the existence of racial wage gaps in the healthcare sector. The study emphasizes the need for structural changes to address these disparities, including policies that promote diversity and inclusion, equal pay for equal work, and transparent salary negotiation processes. Additionally, Khatiwada et al. (2018) provide insights into the racial and ethnic wage gaps within the California Health Care Sector, further emphasizing the urgency of addressing these inequalities.

To tackle wage disparities within specific industries effectively, it is crucial to adopt a multi-faceted approach. Firstly, organizations need to prioritize diversity and inclusion efforts. This includes implementing unbiased hiring practices, establishing mentorship and sponsorship programs for underrepresented employees, and fostering a workplace culture that values and respects diversity.

Transparency in salary negotiations is another critical factor in promoting equity. Employers should strive to provide clear and objective criteria for determining compensation, ensuring that all employees are evaluated fairly and equitably. Companies must also establish mechanisms for employees to report any instances of wage discrimination or bias, creating a safe space for employees to voice their concerns.

Furthermore, education and training play a vital role in dismantling wage gaps. By offering professional development opportunities, organizations can empower their employees, particularly minorities and Black people, with the skills and knowledge needed to thrive in their respective industries. Moreover, companies can partner with educational institutions and community organizations to provide scholarships and internships, creating pathways for underrepresented individuals to enter and excel in these industries.

Ultimately, promoting equity and equality in the workplace requires a collective effort from both individuals and organizations. By addressing the wage gaps within specific industries, such as healthcare, finance, and technology, we can create a more inclusive and fair society. It is imperative for all stakeholders, including employers, policymakers, and individuals, to work together to dismantle these barriers and ensure that everyone has equal opportunities to succeed. Only through these concerted efforts can we truly achieve a more equitable and just society for all.

CHAPTER VI: CONCLUSION

SUMMARY OF FINDINGS

Our study on "The Cost of Inequality: Examining Racial Wage Gaps in Healthcare, Finance, and Technology" provides important findings. This subchapter contains a summary of the findings specifically addressing minorities, particularly Black individuals, and focusing on wage disparities. The findings are based on extensive research and analysis of two key sources: "Racial Wage Gaps in Medicine: Structural, Statistical, and Ethical Considerations" by Kale and Chandra (2020) and "Racial and Ethnic Wage Gaps in the California Health Care Sector" by Khatiwada et al. (2018).

One of the major findings in the healthcare sector is the existence of significant racial wage gaps between Black and white workers. Studies show that Black workers in healthcare occupations, despite having similar qualifications and experiences as their white counterparts, earn significantly lower wages. This wage disparity has serious implications for black healthcare professionals, affecting their financial stability, career growth, and overall well-being.

In the finance industry, the research reveals that Black workers face substantial wage gaps compared to their white counterparts. These gaps persist even when controlling for factors such as education, experience, and job characteristics. The systemic nature of these disparities suggests the presence of structural barriers and discriminatory practices that limit the advancement and economic prosperity of Black individuals within the finance sector.

Similarly, in the technology industry, the wage gaps between Black and white workers are alarming. Despite the increasing demand for skilled technology professionals, Black workers consistently earn lower wages compared to their white counterparts. This disparity not only hampers the economic progress of Black individuals but also perpetuates a lack of diversity and inclusivity within the tech sector.

The findings from these studies expose the perpetual inequalities in the society and highlights the urgent need to address and rectify the racial wage gaps within these specific industries. Policymakers, employers, and society must recognize and combat systemic racism and discriminatory practices that contribute to these wage disparities. Efforts should focus on promoting equal pay for equal work, eliminating bias in hiring and promotion practices, and creating inclusive work environments that foster diversity and equal opportunities. Moreso, the youth must play a significant role in ensuring that they attack each barrier on an individual basis to bridge the gaps.

By understanding the extent of wage gaps between Black and white workers in healthcare, finance, and technology, we can collectively work towards creating a more just and equitable society. It is our hope that this summary of findings serves as a call to action for individuals, organizations, and policymakers to address these disparities and strive for a future where everyone, regardless of their race, can earn fair wages and experience equal opportunities for success.

IMPLICATIONS FOR FUTURE RESEARCH

As we dig deeper into the examination of racial wage gaps in healthcare, finance, and technology, it is imperative to consider the implications for future research. By understanding the underlying factors contributing to these disparities, we can work towards creating a more equitable society for minorities, particularly Black individuals. In healthcare, future research should explore the impact of educational disparities, discrimination, and occupational segregation on wage gaps. By investigating the specific roles within healthcare where wage disparities are most prominent, such as nursing, medical specialties, or administration, we can gain a clearer understanding of the root causes. Additionally, examining the influence of geographic location and the role of unions in negotiating wages could provide valuable insights.

Similarly, in the finance and technology sectors, further research is needed to understand the factors contributing to wage gaps. Exploring the impact of educational attainment, experience, and discrimination in hiring and promotion practices will help identify areas for improvement. Additionally, investigating the role of networking, mentorship, and access to professional development opportunities can provide strategies to address disparities. Overall, future research should aim to uncover the systemic barriers that perpetuate racial wage gaps within specific industries. By focusing on healthcare, finance, and technology, we can gain a comprehensive understanding of the unique challenges faced by Black individuals in these sectors. This research will not only inform policies and practices to reduce wage disparities but will also empower minorities to advocate for fair compensation and equal opportunities. Ultimately, our collective efforts towards addressing these issues will lead to a more inclusive and just society for everyone.

FINAL THOUGHTS AND CALL TO ACTION

Throughout this book, we reviewed the troubling issue of racial wage gaps within specific industries, such as healthcare, finance, and technology. We have examined the structural, statistical, and ethical considerations that contribute to these disparities, shedding light on the injustices faced by minorities, particularly Black individuals, in the workforce. As we reach the end of this journey, it is crucial to reflect on the implications of these findings and the actions we can take to address these inequalities.

The research presented in this book, including the works of Kale and Chandra (2020) and Khatiwada et al. (2018), has unequivocally shown that racial wage gaps persist in sectors such as healthcare, finance, and technology. These gaps not only affect individuals' economic well-being but also perpetuate a cycle of inequality that undermines social cohesion and progress. We must recognize the urgency of this issue and work collectively to bring about meaningful change.

To the minorities and Black people who have been directly impacted by these wage disparities, we want to convey a message of solidarity and empowerment. You are not alone in this struggle, and your experiences are valid. It is important to acknowledge the systemic barriers that perpetuate these wage gaps, including discrimination, biased hiring practices, and limited access to opportunities for advancement. By understanding the root causes, we can begin to challenge and dismantle these barriers together.

To address racial wage gaps within specific industries, we must advocate for policy reforms and institutional changes. This requires the active involvement of both individuals and organizations. As individuals, we can educate ourselves about our rights, demand fair treatment, and support initiatives that promote diversity and inclusion. By utilizing our collective voices, we can create pressure for change and hold institutions accountable for their actions.

Organizations, too, have a responsibility to address racial wage disparities within their sectors. They must commit to implementing transparent and equitable hiring and promotion practices, as well as providing equal access to training and development opportunities. Diversity and inclusion should not be mere buzzwords, but rather integral components of their strategies for success. By fostering a culture that celebrates diversity and rewards merit, organizations can help bridge the wage gaps and create a more just and inclusive society.

In conclusion, the issue of racial wage gaps within specific industries demands our attention and action. To achieve a fair and equitable society, we must confront the systemic barriers that perpetuate these disparities. The result of these inequalities can be summarized in some of the key findings in the studies cited in this book, and particularly, the following by Thomas & Valentine, of the Aurrera Health Group, titled, "Health Disparities by Race and Ethnicity in California: Pattern of Inequity. Thomas & Valentine (2021) found that Black Californians had the shortest life expectancy at 75.1 years…The Black population in California experienced the highest death rates from breast, cervical, colorectal, lung, and prostate cancer among all racial and ethnic groups. Black Californians experienced the highest rates of prenatal and postpartum depressive symptoms; low-risk, first-birth cesareans; preterm births; low-birthweight births; infant mortality; and maternal mortality.

By standing together, demanding change, and holding institutions accountable, we can work towards a future where all individuals, regardless of their race, have equal opportunities and fair compensation in the workplace. Let us not be silent, but rather be catalysts for change.

REFERENCES

Alfonseca, K (September 2021). Generational wealth implications: Black and Latino-owned homes are more likely to be undervalued. Retrieved from https://abcnews.go.com/US/generational-wealth-implications-black-latino-owned-homes-undervalued/story?id=80208131

American Psychological Association. (2021, October 7). For Black students, unfairly harsh discipline can lead to lower grades [Press release]. Retrieved from https://www.apa.org/news/press/releases/2021/10/black-students-harsh-discipline

Anderson, D (April 2021). The Price of Racial Bias: Homes in Black Neighborhoods Are Valued at an Average of $46,000 Less Than Similar Homes in White Neighborhoods
Retrieved from
https://www.redfin.com/news/undervaluation-homes-black-versus-white-neighborhoods/

Brewer, Z. (November 2020). Why waiters give Black customers poor service. Retrieved from https://theconversation.com/why-waiters-give-black-customers-poor-service-149210

Berdejó, C. (2017). Criminalizing Race: Racial Disparities in Plea-Bargaining. Boston College Law Review, 59(4), 1187-1242. Retrieved from https://papers.ssrn.com/sol3/papers.cfm?abstract_id=3036726

Berdejó, C., & Angwin, J. (2017). When Race Tips the Scales in Plea Bargaining. The Marshall Project. Retrieved from https://www.themarshallproject.org/2017/10/23/when-race-tips-the-scales-in-plea-bargaining

Brown, R (February 2023). Why do innocent people end up pleading guilty? (2023). New York Daily News. Retrieved from https://www.nydailynews.com/2023/02/10/why-do-innocent-people-end-up-pleading-guilty/

Connley, C (May 2021). Why Black workers still face a promotion and wage gap that's costing the economy trillions. Retrieved from https://www.cnbc.com/2021/04/16/black-workers-face-promotion-and-wage-gaps-that-cost-the-economy-trillions.html

Delgado, M & Ortegren, F (April 2023). America's Housing Inequality and the Racial Wealth Divide Retrieved from https://listwithclever.com/research/2021-housing-inequality-report/

DeSilver, D., Lipka, M. & Fahmy, D. (June 2020). 10 things we know about race and policing in the U.S. Retrieved from https://www.pewresearch.org/short-reads/2020/06/03/10-things-we-know-about-race-and-policing-in-the-u-s/

Dunn, R (n.d). Racial Disparities in Traffic Ticketing Retrieved from https://crimeandjusticeresearchalliance.org/rsrch/racial-disparities-in-traffic-ticketing/

Fair Trials. (2018). Plea Bargaining: An International Perspective. Retrieved from https://www.fairtrials.org/sites/default/files/publication_pdf/Plea-Bargaining-Report.pdf

Federal Reserve History. (2023). Redlining. Retrieved from https://www.federalreservehistory.org/essays/redlining

Fields, J, M, Perry, M, A & Donoghoe, M (August 2023). How the property tax system harms Black homeowners and widens the racial wealth gap. Retrieved from https://www.brookings.edu/articles/how-the-property-tax-system-harms-black-homeowners-and-widens-the-racial-wealth-gap/

Flores, S & Pinkerton, B (August 2021). Addressing inequalities in society. Retrieved from https://www.sportanddev.org/latest/news/addressing-inequalities-society

GAO (2018). K-12 Education: Discipline Disparities for Black Students, Boys, and Students with Disabilities. Retrieved from https://www.gao.gov/products/gao-18-258

Horowitz, J.M., Hurst, K., Braga, D (June 2023). Views of the treatment of Black people in America https://www.pewresearch.org/social-trends/2023/06/14/views-of-the-treatment-of-black-people-in-america/

Ince, S (October 2022). Race and Exonerations: Why Black Defendants Are More Likely To Be Wrongfully Convicted. (2022). Syracuse Law Review. Retrieved from https://lawreview.syr.edu/race-and-exonerations-why-black-defendants-are-more-likely-to-be-wrongfully-convicted/

Jones, J. M & Lloyd, C (July 2021). Black Americans' Reports of Mistreatment Steady or Higher. Retrieved from https://www.amren.com/news/2021/07/black-americans-reports-of-mistreatment-steady-or-higher/

Lemerise, U (May 2016). YOUTH AND INEQUALITY: Time to support youth as agents of their own future. Retrieved from https://www-cdn.oxfam.org/s3fs-public/file_attachments/bp-youth-inequality-global-120816-en_0.pdf

Losey, S (May 2016). Race and the Air Force: The truth about how minorities get promoted. Retrieved from https://www.airforcetimes.com/news/your-air-force/2016/03/01/race-and-the-air-force-the-truth-about-how-minorities-get-promoted/

Minooee, S (2023). Discrimination during childbirth among black birthing people predicts postpartum care utilization Evidence-Based Nursing Published Online First: 12 December 2023. doi: 10.1136/ebnurs-2023-103849. Retrieved from: https://ebn.bmj.com/content/early/2023/12/12/ebnurs-2023-103849

NCSL (May 2022). Racial and Ethnic Disparities in the Criminal Justice System

Retrieved from https://www.ncsl.org/civil-and-criminal-justice/racial-and-ethnic-disparities-in-the-criminal-justice-system

Price-Mitchell (June 2022). How to Help Young People Fight Racial Inequality. Retrieved from https://www.psychologytoday.com/us/blog/the-moment-youth/202006/how-help-young-people-fight-racial-inequality

Rezal, A (2021). The Racial Makeup of America's Prisons. Retrieved from https://www.usnews.com/news/best-states/articles/2021-10-13/report-highlights-staggering-racial-disparities-in-us-incarceration-rates

Roque, L., Khattar, R., & Pathak, A (March 2022). Black Men and the U.S. Economy: How the Economic Recovery Is Perpetuating Systemic Racism. Retrieved from https://www.americanprogress.org/article/black-men-and-the-u-s-economy-how-the-economic-recovery-is-perpetuating-systemic-racism/

Smart, T (May 2021). Report Finds Racism Prevalent in the Workplace (usnews.com). Retrieved from https://www.usnews.com/news/national-news/articles/2021-05-24/report-finds-racism-prevalent-in-the-workplace

SpringerLink. (2022). Discrimination in Credit. Retrieved from https://link.springer.com/referenceworkentry/10.1007/978-981-33-4016-9_14-1

The Associated Press (April 2018). A look at claims of racial bias in US restaurants. Retrieved from https://apnews.com/general-news-3e20d51972fc4bca9136e30c3839e514

Thomas, M & Valentine, A (October 2021). Health Disparities by Race and Ethnicity in California: Pattern of Inequity. Retrieved from chrome-extension://efaidnbmnnnibpcajpcglclefindmkaj/https://www.chcf.org/wp-content/uploads/2021/10/DisparitiesAlmanacRaceEthnicity2021.pdf

UN (August 2021). Young people are at the forefront of the fight against racial discrimination. Retrieved from
https://www.ohchr.org/en/stories/2021/08/young-people-are-forefront-fight-against-racial-discrimination

UNICEF (June 2020). Five actions you can take against racism and discrimination. Retrieved from
https://www.voicesofyouth.org/blog/five-actions-you-can-take-against-racism-and-discrimination

www.ingramcontent.com/pod-product-compliance
Lightning Source LLC
Chambersburg PA
CBHW051619010526
44119CB00009B/209